to the loved ones i have lost
and to those who still love me
today, thank you for inspiring
me to become something more
than another human who stays
the same because change and
losing yourself all over again
is too damn hard to deal with.
Thank you for making me this
way, a Troubadour.

-karnes-

TROUBADOUR

-Prose

-Poetry

-Stories

Written By

-karnes-

Chapter 1

-Stories-

This is my second book like this. The kind you simply allow your mind and current life situation to write for you. It all comes in phases and I am thankful my brain works this way. It has its own process, its own breaking point when the energy overwhelms my body. That is the only time I know when to shut down for the day and step away from it all. This year may have been the most difficult one yet for several reasons. Nothing horrible took place or happened, knock on wood, but it just seems to have had such a slow and tedious beginning to it, with more layers being added onto it ever since. It feels like the wettest blanket has been heaped and pushed onto me with no escaping it. This summer has been the hottest one on record for Texas, and most of the country I am sure. August will be here tomorrow, which is the hottest month for us down here. I cannot even begin to imagine the intensity and heat indexes for it. We have had a steady temperature of over 110 degrees ever since June. The grass is as brown as death can look at times. The clouds have been shy and dormant for the most part. There is never enough shade to keep the house cool and A/C from coming on. We have kept it at 86 degrees during the day and 82 degrees at night. I am and have always been thankful for the way I can suffer and suffer willingly in order to be okay in the end. Today is August 1ˢᵗ, and with it, a full super moon will be out tonight. The second one of this year. At the end of the month on the 30ᵗʰ, there will be another one, a blue moon. I can only hope this month is kind to us all and allows us to step further into this year with a more conscious heart and soul. I feel as if I have been at a crossroads in my life the last four or five years. When I moved back here to Texas to help my father out, I had no idea exactly how long I would actually be here. But I did know for certain, once I felt a push or pull to go somewhere again, I would. That hasn't transpired or happened just yet unfortunately. Unlike the last time when I went to Utah, I knew it was where I was meant to be. Maybe it's because I haven't had any road-trips the last several years. The ones I have been on so far, I have already visited those places before. I haven't been out of the state of Texas in years. I can feel my soul dying a bit more the longer I am unable to make it out of here. You know the feeling you get when you stay in one place for too long and you become suffocated, caged, turned inside out, and your entire being becomes a suffering object, twisting, curling, and knotting up in adventure-less behavior. Maintaining a positive outlook on life isn't the easiest thing to do when you feel such a negative pull from the place you are in and the environment around you. I can feel the anxieties from my father, which I know he doesn't enjoy having, but I pick up on the slightest mood changes and swings of anyone near or close to me. The energies never lie, nor do the ways you feel it surround you, absolutely overwhelming every particle of your existence. Some days, I feel myself lined up against the brick and patterned walls, patiently awaiting whatever firing squad is pulled up and ready to do what they need to do. The no way out feeling is real. The impending doom sitting back and watching its soldiers take your life away from you before you have a chance to improve any aspect of it. I do my best with the balance though. I drive into town just enough to escape being locked up in this house all day with only my father around. He stays on the couch and watches his TV when he isn't outside watering or working out. We both have a similar routine, which if you live with someone and basically mirror their actions before the sun reaches 12 o'clock, you will eventually become each and every one of their behaviors. I learned that by watching and being around my mother during my entire childhood. But these behaviors are such a bipolar opposite from then. I do not take it as a bad thing. I simply take it for what it is and move forward with my day. Whether I am typing, writing, reading, or creating something new for my website, I am constantly moving with my mind or body. The exercising never ceases. To hold up in this life, we must nurture ourselves in whatever ways we can, whenever we can. I will be thirty-eight next month. I swear I had just written about that not too long ago, and here I am now, already closer to forty. I've never given growing older much thought, because at the end of the day, it is something we all do if we are lucky. There was a death yesterday, Angus Cloud. I never watched the show, Euphoria, but he was one of the main actors in it and probably the most beloved in a lot of ways. I read he wasn't even an actor before the show. Somehow, a talent agency found him while he was working some regular job in Los Angeles. His father had recently passed away, which the grief alone could have killed him. From what I have read from other people's first hand accounts, that is what happened. The investigation has been an ongoing thing for a few days now, so I won't write about it as if I have the answers as to why, but it was a medical emergency and he was found dead upon arrival to the house. He was only twenty-five. It is incredibly sad to read about someone so young taking their own life, especially when I know from experience how it feels in a lot of ways with my suicide attempt back in 2009. I know how devastated my parents and brothers were when I had to make the phone calls to each of them from ICU, then from rehab when I got there. It breaks my heart that so many young and adult men in particular, feel as though they have no other option. When having to ask or reach out for help is still considered taboo in so many ways, more of us will go down that rabbit hole, because we are judged so harshly for not being able to keep it together when everything around us is fucking falling apart. Too often, we all find ourselves in the cross-hairs of life with no options left, or at least we think it is the case. When all it takes is to reach out and tell someone, "I am not having a good day. I am not feeling mentally strong today." I know it is difficult to bow down to that hurt and grief, giving it the power to actually impact your entire life and world. To be helpless is not what we want at all. The alternative is giving ourselves all the power we can by making the choice that we want. However illogical or logical that is, I feel as though we will never solve the issue of mental health as long as we continue fixating on the endgame of it and not the steps needed to be taken to correct such matters. I can only hope he is at peace now and reunites with his father as he thought he would once he decided to take his own life. There was also another death just a few days before that.

Paul Reubens passed away from cancer at the age of seventy. It was a battle he was fighting alone for the most part including family members, and they were the only ones who knew. He never spoke about it publicly and even wrote a statement before he did die. He was an actor who played Pee-Wee Herman, a childhood staple for me growing up. I would watch his show every weekend, Pee-Wee's Playhouse. I had the pillows, the pajamas, and the movie which we had on VHS at the time. I am sure my mom still has it somewhere at the house if it wasn't broken already by me watching it as often as I did. I spoke about it on Instagram recently, and how the show helped me in my childhood with all the chaos going on around me. It gave my imagination room to expand and think outside the box. I believe I was four or five at the time the show came out and then a year or two older once I finally watched the movie. Tony Bennett passed away before those two did, so the 'three" scheme was correct again. I remember being a kid and my mother telling me about the death by threes. Ever since then, if one celebrity dies, two more will be close behind. The universe is a strange place, but all answers are found within the numbers that we all come across. The defined definition of life is a patterned sequence. Maybe it has to do with the energy alone or it is just the fate that exists which a lot of people do not believe in. Lucky for me, I find myself to be a believer in a lot of things others aren't and or could never grasp. I am happy I am that way. It allows me to see things differently, with a more unparalleled existence so to speak. My younger brother and I will be going to Italy this coming October. My father has always wanted to go, and it has been a place and area of the world that has been within me and on my mind since I was old enough to know what other places were out there, besides the United States. I remember doing school projects on it and getting all the information I could, then watching every single mob/mafia movie I could. It has fascinated me ever since. My father will be seventy in November, so it is an early birthday gift from us to him. I believe it is his number one bucket list item. His affinity and love for

Italy goes way back. To the cigars, wine, cheese, bread, culture, and scenery, it is second to none for him. Every year, my father and I watch the Giro d'Italia. It is a professional cycling race that takes place in Italy and goes all throughout the country. It is a twenty-one day stage race, which if you have ever watched it or any of the Grand Tours of cycling, you would instantly fall in love with every country they put these races in. It's been a dream of ours to get over there, and thanks to my younger brother, it is coming to fruition. I have dreamt of places and adventures my entire life. I am a traveling dream of a human I suppose. I have never been happy in one place for too long, but when I was in Utah, I could have lived out my days happily there. But life isn't always in agreement with what we what. It ultimately decides for us, just like with love and death. It has its own final and ultimate say in everything we do, touch, and hold onto. I do know when we get to Italy, none of us will want to come back. At least that is the synopsis from the feeling I already have about getting over there. I will write every day I am there, and hopefully create the best of what I have been trying to do ever since I began this journey. Today is Tuesday Another 110 plus degree day. The brown grass is everywhere here now. It has taken over this part of the state. I cannot recall the last time we actually had rain. My father goes outside a few times a week and waters it, along with the holes that come about by the drought we are in. It is long-winded work to say the least. I called my dentist today to tell him about one of my teeth not aligning after the last visit in April. They forgot to give me my upper tray before I left. Now, it looks like I will need Invisalign again, as well as getting my implant fixed while I am there. It has been loose for a few weeks now. Funny thing is, I have barely chewed on anything using the left side of my mouth. The things I have eaten, have been soft food for the most part. Rice, spaghetti, and beans. A mostly liquid diet for me since the tooth became loosened. When the temperature gets as warm as it does like this, your appetite goes dormant. You do all you can to not sweat, so you hydrate as often as possible and do not move unless you have to. Suffering like this is a choice by the way. Money is and has been tight for the last several years after my father lost his job in 2018. I do all I can to make whatever money possible to help out. Maybe one day we won't have to suffer like this and can actually turn the air down below eighty-six for a change. I feel as though it has been my entire life, a true suffering. Between being born sick, being raised by an alcoholic mother, the list goes on, but it does feel as if I have known nothing but suffering for the sake of my own life being what it is today. I have a twisted mind and a dark one at that. The more brutal the life around me is, the more up to the challenge I find myself being. I remember when I was in boot camp and having drill instructors in my face yelling or while out running PT, the louder they got, the more my fire burned. The motivation is entirely unique to me I am sure. Not everyone enjoys that type of discipline. Fortunately and unfortunately, I was raised by it and on it. I was entirely used to it by the time I enlisted, so the more screaming there was, the better I preformed.

I am an odd one without question, but I own it and speak openly about it. My struggles made me, just as they do with anyone who braves it and makes it out more of who they were and needed to be to endure such aspects of life. Some days, I have no idea where these pages will take me. I can only hope they lead me to more healing, a better understanding of myself and the role I play in the grand scheme of things. I do my best to give my soul the upmost freedom when it comes to writing. Flowing in and out of whatever state of mind I need to be in and or finds me. I have learned the more you look and search for defined words, feelings, and emotions, the less you will gestate them. We are only as vulnerable as we know how to be. I am thankful to have been born with this heart and mind that only knows that. I am unashamed of who I am and of my story. It matters to me, and as long as it does, I will not stop sharing it. If anything I write can help someone feel less inundated, I have done my duty for that specific day. If I can endure this torturous life which finds me begging for answers, I know I am where I need to be.

Chapter 2

-Poetry/Prose-

No Reason Needed

i don't need a publicized day to love you or to buy you flowers. each day is a reason to give you my best effort. each day is a reason to give you unconditional and unannounced love. to the way you open your eyes like two moons giving birth to new feelings, you make me want to eat you alive and save the marks and bruises you give me to remember how lost humans can get if you allow them to go beyond their boundaries. to the way your legs open for me, i am begging to be ruined. to the way our bodies go from wall to wall, we are making our own foundation, which will withstand any pressure we feel to be more ravaging. all the way to being intent on destroying each other just so we can spend more time considering how to hold the other when we are finished. there is a certain way love looks to those who are vulnerable and soulfully whole. you and i get there without needing to touch flesh and bone. we combust upon the first and slightest of heart contact. nights can be unbelievably lonely at times. especially when all that can hold you

are the memories of what used to be and when
these cold sheets used to burn with a such a fire,
it would light up the crowded night sky.
for some, love will never be enough. but for
others, it will always be everything. that's the
maddening part about life. it is the thought of
before it all ended, the precursor to how it is
today, and where it all fell off the rails. you do
your best to not allow it to eat at you until you
are nothing more than a memory to yourself.
you can be in bed for days with such images
and feelings without ever being able to move.
you surrender all hope to the light that has
found you, and you relish in the darkness that
encapsulates you, because at least there, it feels
as if you can be closer to something that knows
you better. i remember so much, it physically
hurts my heart, lungs, and every other organ
that once knew you. there is only so much
we can do when we get entirely attached to
someone like that. someone who becomes both
entities of love and death. someone who makes
you forget about anything before that moment
that may have caused you harm. you never see
an end to it until it is too late. by then, you are

combusting into anger, rage, and fear of never having it again, because you know you won't. you know you may never be around someone like that again. it happened to me, and only once was i able to get it back, but it was with the same person. i always believed in forever, be it with love or any other tangible existence. i grew up in my own head, my own beastly mind, a space of freedom, but also creating a lifetime's worth of wishes. a few showed up as i thought they would, and only a single time, did it show up as someone's face. i am haunted by it now. i cannot look at anyone and not see it, not witness the smile that changed the course of my life. i do not know if i will ever get it back, but i look to the moon as often as i can, and ask her to return it back to me, begging it to return it back to me safely, with an admiration of a homeward-bound feeling. i barely got to spend a week overall with her in person, and within that week, i knew i could never not be with her in this life, while writing her in all of my books. it has to fucking count for some sort of balanced approach to living a good life right?

No List Needed

i remember being a kid and having this monster list i would always end up giving to my parents for Christmas. when i find myself thinking back on those days, i feel so bad making my mom and dad think that i "needed" more things than what i already had. as the years have gone by, one after the other, i have begun to realize having everything is something i never actually needed, but at the time, it was the only thing i wanted. another year is about to pass me, and all i had on my list this time, was to be happy. that's all i wanted. to see how this year has blessed me with so much, i can truly say, i've already received everything on my list.

Covenant

you will never really know what could happen once you take your first step into something that makes you completely uncomfortable and terrified, making you doubt everything you thought you once knew. i am working on my second step now. i cannot wait to see where it leads me in the coming New Year. day one without smoking. i made a promise to two humans who i told i would quit. you and i. i am not going to break a promise of which i have looked you in the heart and whispered to your soul. that is not who i am, even if you are away from me now, the bond and pact is still as evident as your absence is.

The Next Full Year

a new year brings new-sprung opportunities and chances to do everything you couldn't do in the years leading up until now. go do them and smile at those who told you, you couldn't. live for yourself, but love everyone you can. it's ironic when people deliberately think they have everything, because their money can buy anything. sometimes, it is those with absolutely nothing who will forever be happy. they will never understand the difference, and i hope i never have to either. we are still several months from the next full year, but i always find myself somewhere in the middle of past and old ones, discovering words and emotions left by its parents for me to find and write about.

Two Forty-Three

**"did i love her too much, not enough,
or did i even love her at all."**

i closed my bleary eyes, drifted off into a sobering dream, trying to come up with an answer. i awoke around two forty-three that morning, only to realize the answer was to love her more than my heart had ever loved anyone else. not because it was the way, but because it was what we both deserved. i had never fully bought into the idea of forever with anyone, and when i was on the precipice, they showed me precisely why my heart always remained beating, stranded in halves. we owe ourselves not only our best, but the best from someone else when all-in is the epitome of life itself.

The Other Side Of Summer

you have always been the other side of summer, fall's first light and a million embers all coming from the four agreements of life. i could tell you that you were different, but i am searching for something you have not heard before, as if you marched out of hell itself to bring with you all the ones who were never given a chance to live before. one by one, you gave all of us a reason to run with the wolves again.

When You Know, You Know

maybe that is all we will be, some paused moment in someone else's life when the only thing perfect was everything, because we surrendered to the belief of already having it all. i do not pray anymore, but i do speak things out loud so the universe can hear them as clear as my vocal chords can make it out to be. i will never give up on the perfection of laying with you on some throw blanket on the floor, looking at each other in a blindly haze, recognizing that our day is being today, tomorrow, and whatever is left for us to live together. i swear to you, it has kept me up thirty-seven years, going on thirty-eight.

Humanly Sense

give into this wild and it will give back to you. there are times to risk it all for what you want. be that for yourself now. risk every fucking piece of your worried heart for a chance of never having it hurt again in any capacity. give into the makings of complete and fulfilling wonderment. there is nothing quite like falling for the feelings you cannot describe with any humanly sense being made of it.

Therapeutic Teachings

punching keys with over thirty years of built-up sadness and anger is just one of my ways to release who i was. i can still hear the faint cries from the innocent child without a childhood who made do with silence as a friend because he knew at least then, no one was after him or trying to get him to assist in their misery or games. i feel sorry for my typewriter at times. there isn't anyone in the world who could hear these stories and have the capacity or love to stay, but here we are, still trying to get to know one another all these years later. here i am, still trying to get to know myself all these years later. what a full circle moment it has become. what semi-circle i once was.

Moving Target

there is no explanation for what i do. i feel the vibes, the energy, and go where they take me. i walk and can feel the stories of Mother Earth, as if she was reading every human a story from a time before, but not everyone is listening. there is extraordinary brilliancy in being weird, strange, an outcast to the masses. we are too busy with things in front of us to pay attention to the love we are walking on. what a wasteful life it is for some of us who are constructed in the beliefs of those who have never crawled before to get back to the center of it all.

Hopeful When Defeat Closes In

i know you have your place you go to when the world gets too loud and your heart gets too heavy to stay inside of your chest. you are the best version of comfort, and i can only hope one day you feel it for yourself. others may call you crazy and every other wild word they have learned along the way, but you remain the brightest eyes in whatever space you occupy. your hands still tremble and shake from time to time, but you are as steady as any rhythm this earth could hold. some days, you feel so lost, you cannot decide which room to cry in, which leads you out the door and onto a piece of sidewalk where you write your name in chalk just to remind yourself we all have a place within this world. i hope your wonder survives, because it is the most beautiful thing about you. it will take you everywhere you need to go if you can relinquish the control for once. you and your worries have grown up together, which created the opaque look in your eyes. you do not get out much anymore, and when you do, there is no escaping what you are constantly trying to run from. i hope the second-guessing doesn't weigh you down to the point of crushing your child-like spirit. i hope your laughter stays the same in every room you find. i hope it is as boisterous as the sun and moon speaking love into all things.

Ornament

i am still looking for my solid patch of earth. my significant secret to keep. my whimsy whisper to savor. my third eye to engross each and every fiber of truth and reality. my own heart jumps at whatever adventure comes next. my life seems to be intertwined with stars and bones, all trying with their mightiness to become one. the next time something graces my path and ignites my soul, i hope i explode with a magical sense of calm, but enough madness to try it all again to excavate the first time feeling of being separated from survivor and angrily constructed.

Why It All Means More

i never wish to know another hand that is not
yours or lips that do not part as yours do
when they tell me, good night, good morning,
and how much you have missed me when i was
only a few feet away. you are the only reason
i know how to wake up and roll to where you
are to begin each and every day of my second
chance revival of living without ache and guilt
for being happy, for having you here with me.

Age Is Faceless

i know you may never see me again and i may never hold you the same as i once did when that is all i knew how to do with these arms. i know without hesitation, i will love you this much and all the same as i did before whenever you are sixty and feeling seventy-five. there is an age gap between us. i remember vividly the first time you told me how much it scared you. you never once asked me why not be with someone younger, but you did ask me, why you. i told you i was attracted to women older than me. though when we first spoke and i saw a photo of you, i had no idea you were the age of which you told me. i simply knew and felt the connection to you was something i had never felt before, and that was with me being engaged once before a decade plus ago. i also knew it was worth pursuing, that you were worth all the time and energy i had and could give you. when it comes to love for me, your name is the first and only word out of my mouth. your body, all smiles and golden skin, is the only vision i have wherever i am when someone asks me if i have ever been in love.

When A Loss Becomes A Victory

death used to know my name, and now
it dreams of me, thinking about how
beautiful a memory can be once you
lose what you once had and it never
returns to you in this life or the next.

A December True Blue

i can feel you through the shine and butterflies, all encompassing as the moon talks and tells its stories about you. you are one of the free ones, a true capture of the light and freedom. you were born for the impossible, for the wildness inside of your heart. you are the rarity the cosmos speaks of, a million moons inside of a human's heart. a keeper of all things precious and delicate, you walk slowly to take in and show appreciation for all of the living things which give you life. i know at times it can be difficult trying to find your footing, but for an earth angel like you, your wings will always set you apart from everything. your name is holy, a setting sun on every horizon. a flower child, a moon child, a brave wild thing, you are. i hope you never forget all of the dreams you dream and all of the places they take you. you may not feel as though you will make it to your destination. but that is the beauty of the journey. life only asks us to be present, and that is something you simply cannot struggle with. eyes of fire, you are. a true blue with a pronounced craving and ache, it's you.

Chapter 3

-Stories-

Today is Friday, and with that, another 110 plus degree finds us here in this part of Texas. I have been staying busy with the next book I have coming out next week, while taking time to do work in this one. It feels good to be able to space out my time on here and not give it all away within one sitting. I am still learning how to do the same with my personal life. I am a giver at heart, and with that, I typically give out more than I ever get back in return. My childhood molded me into becoming that. It wasn't until about five or six years ago that I stumbled upon the word, empath. I know it was the cause for a lot of self-sabotage and self-inflicted chaos within my own life. I did all I could to survive as a young kid. I eventually acquired the ability to block out and black out certain parts of my life over time. It didn't help that I did every drug known to man almost and drank myself into blackouts to escape the pain and torture I felt. There are days when it feels as though I cannot write enough or get out everything I am trying or wanting to say. This brain of mine never shuts off. The thoughts never stop coming to me and asking if it is okay to use them in the writings. I was unsure if I wanted to add this to this book, but this is how we all become more vulnerable, by sharing what we think we shouldn't. I have been dealing with anxiety for over a decade now. Progressively and over time, it has gotten worse I feel like. I was on Paxil for six months back in 2020 after the pandemic hit full force. I went to urgent care, all masked up and the doctors were all masked up as well. It was strange to say the least, but I was able to walk in and get checked out. I told him what I was going through and feeling. It was the first time I had gone to a medical facility since my panic attack episode in 2013. I went to the window and got my paper work to fill out. Once the doctor came in, he began asking me about it word for word. I wore a short sleeve T-shirt that day. There are a few parts of my arms where you can still see the scars from my suicide attempt in 2009, even with my full sleeve tattoos. Fate would have it, he saw them, and asked me what happened. I told him with shame almost. It was the first time in years I had to explain what had happened. He said, "why didn't you write that down." I told him I wasn't here for that and those scars had nothing to do with my current situation. He went forward with more questions after that as doctors tend to do. He prescribed me with a low dosage of Paxil, which is an anxiety medication. Before that, I had issues with my liver, which I got checked out in 2017 after having pains there for two years. My pain tolerance is extremely high and it has caused me to endure an absurd amount of pain over the years. I am good at compartmentalizing, which isn't always the best thing for us to do, but it is a self-defense mechanism I suppose. I found some OTC medication for my pain in the liver area after going to radiology for them to examine me further. They found a few spots on it and wanted me to go to a hospital in Corpus Christi, which is about a fifteen minute drive from here. After taking the pills I found, the pain subsided and I didn't go to get checked out. The urgent care visit cost me $200 for him to tell me I had anxiety. Something I already knew I had. The medical field is such a scam when it comes to that, but I do not carry medical insurance. It is ridiculously high, somewhere in the neighborhood of five to six hundred dollars for me. I cannot afford the proper one I need, so I pay out of pocket for all of it. It isn't the worst thing, because they give you some sort of discount for it. The radiology appointment cost me $300 dollars for the scan and the doctor visit which lead me there cost me an additional $150. On top of all of that, I have had my blood work done a few times and each one of those are almost one hundred dollars. All of that to say this, I began experiencing pain on the left side of my body near the stomach or pancreas, not sure which organ it is, but it is an every day thing. Some days, it hurts worse than others, but I seem to manage it the best I can. That situation began the day Kobe Bryant died in the helicopter crash with his daughter and others inside of it. It was an instant pain right there on the left side. I have been dealing with it now for over three years. I do not know what is wrong with it, but it causes my anxiety to become worse and it is extremely hard for me to stay seated or in one spot for too long if I am not moving. It doesn't hurt when I am working out. It hurts after I eat, and especially after I am done for the day and resting. It is impossible to find a comfortable spot after three or four in the afternoon. I do not know if I am too scared to get it checked out or if I am just stubborn and do not want to pay what I think it will cost to get it checked out. I find myself laying down in my bean bag chair, massaging that side of my body for the rest of the night. I can sleep perfectly fine though, which I think if it was something in dire need of getting checked out, it would become worrisome at night like most pains and illnesses do. All I know is, I will have to eventually get it looked at, because there is no way I can properly function like this for the rest of my life. The anxiety it gives me alone is the only reason I would go. As I mentioned before, we are heading to Italy this fall, and I am already dreading the plane trip over there. I had never been anxious before of flying or sitting still or anything close to those things. My first plane ride was when I was six years old. We flew from Dallas to Sacramento to go see my father and stay with him in Los Banos, California for what I think was half a year. I've flown a hundred times since that day, and more times than not, I was alone doing it. The last time I flew somewhere was in 2017 to go to Arizona. I rented a car and flew out of San Antonio. The drive was brutal because I believe I had separation anxiety from living with my father so long. I made it there though. I was borderline freaking out on the plane ride. Thankfully, it was less than a three hour trip to land in Phoenix. I have no idea where the anxiety came from and why it has been as present as it has been, but I will never take pills again. They only turn you into a zombie, an nonfunctional spectacle, and make everyday life almost nonstructural. It rids you of your humanity and turns you into someone you do not recognize. Add to that, the Big Pharma gets wealthier, and I am never going to give them my own money for something that can be treated through meditation and other natural ways. Whatever it is I am experiencing, I know will sort itself out and I will be okay. I have never publicly spoken about it and wanted to share it here, with you the reader, so you know how much of someone we barely know and how often looking from the outside, we all seem normal and okay. I do know I will have to do something though before flying out in a few months. That has been life for me the last three plus years, while also doing my best to be as humanly made as possible. I am working on a lot of projects these days. When I first began this journey in the summer of 2014, I simply wanted to journal my thoughts in a way I thought could help me along with those whomever found my words to read. I had no idea it would become this, but I did know writing has always been my purpose and call to life. It took me a little longer to arrive at that affirmation, but I did. I also began writing to get someone I loved back in my life. It did what it was supposed to do and she finally noticed my writing and began reading more of it and commenting on it. We got back in touch over the Facebook eventually. But it didn't last that long because she was seeing someone at the time who later turned out to become her future husband. We kept in contact and were actually going to meet up, but she got pregnant and that was that. I cut-off all communication with her after I found out. To say this has been a beautiful experience overall, I would have to say it has. Though in a lot of ways, it also has caused me grief, heartache, and depression. I am coming up on being eight years sober, which will be here this October. I quit drinking after a blackout episode that scared my younger brother and brought me to terms that I was a functioning alcoholic, as well as being my own worst enemy. I did it for myself and to provide myself the longevity I deserved, as well as a true happiness for the first time in my life. At the beginning of it, I was afraid I wouldn't be able to write as well or the same as I did while I drinking every day and night. I thought it was my superpower and something I needed to bring up the thoughts and feelings I had been feeling, saved up, and came across in my daily life. It took me a while to figure that process out, but I got there. If you are struggling with a substance or just in life, please know it does get better as long as we want it to be better. We are the catalyst for everything and anything that happens in our lives. Nothing happens without our actions or say so. I firmly believe that. We can try and blame fate or destiny, but we are the captain of it all. It sinks or stays afloat with us at the helm. If we do not take responsibility and accountability for our lives, no one else will, and if they do, just know they are not there to help you with it. They are there to fuck it up in some way and get you off course, because our demons are ours to suffocate and leave behind. Of course we can ask for help and seek opinions of others whom we trust, but we are the grounds for where it all takes place. No one knows what we are going through or dealing with except ourselves. Trust in that and you will never go astray. I am almost done writing on here for the day. I am about to eat a couple of hot dogs and a cauliflower pizza. Sounds amazing doesn't it? My eating habits and choices have always been a bit of a mixed bag, but I am willing to eat anything at least once and try something different should I get the opportunity to do so. It is one of my most favorite things to do when there is time for it. I am not a big eater. I do not know if i even eat 2,000 calories a day. I do know if I am at my grandmother's house, I will easily eat that before lunch. I have never been one to eat a lot, unless I am at a restaurant and there are multiple choices for me to decide on. I will have my coffee with creamer in the morning, protein shake after working out, then I have lunch/dinner around two or three, then snack around five in the evening. Since I have been living with my dad, we eat when he is hungry, and being the age he is, dinner is early, and I eat and snack my way through the rest of the day. I have been journaling a lot more because I bought a Whoop a few months ago. It gives you an option to journal each morning, which I do. I allow myself to speak kindly to myself. First thing in the morning, I believe it is important to set the tone for the day with words of love and acceptance for where we are, who we are, and where it is we find ourselves upon waking. It has helped me with my writings I type up, but I still have my bad days when nothing feels as if it is going my way. Such is life though. We all seem to find that hole we dig and crawl into when things feel as though they are the same in and same out every single fucking day. It isn't depression for me. It is me battling my inability to focus on the task at hand and be more vigilant with my own needs and desires. Again, living with your father or parent(s) doesn't help when you have so much you want to do in this life, and it also doesn't help when you are the only one with a vehicle. I have never quite felt like I was cleansing in concrete, while remaining shackled, as if I were some imprisoned version of my present self. With all that being said, I know how lucky I am to have my father still, and for that matter, both parents. I do not know if that is something I could have said fifteen or twenty years ago because of how much resentment I felt towards them. But with all things said, we live and learn, all while understanding everything constantly changes. I love my father. He has done so many things for me, whom without, I could not and would not be alive today or doing what I am doing. Each day, I get to go outside and run on the track while he walks his five to six miles. He suffers as well as I do, and suffering runs in the family with certainty. Growing up not being super wealthy or having every single thing my friends or everyone else had ultimately gave me a perspective and an understanding that to be without materialistic items was not the end of the world. My father has taught me a lot about life since being around him and observing him daily it seems for the past decade. I hope I have been able to show and teach him a few things as well with the way I am, along with the persistence I have for my workouts and mindset of being this way. With his age creeping towards seventy, there is a new found hurried sense for me to hep him as much as I can while he still has his health and able to do things on his own. There was a time several months ago, I would run on my treadmill and he would walk on the track. He was usually out of the house before seven-thirty in the morning. I was never too far behind, but he would leave sticky notes on the table and tell me he was out there. I remember thinking how much I would miss those notes if something ever happened to him. It was a grand way to begin my day knowing he was okay and out and about. I recently broke my treadmill after three plus years of running on it, which forced me to begin my running again outside. My body isn't what it once was when I was in the Marine Corps, running on open roads and pavement for countless miles at a time. I have put my body through hell since I was old enough to be outside on my own. My knees, lower back, hips, ankles, and feet have just about been run into the ground with the hard labor I've done along with me being in the Marines doing grunt work. I was once able to run three miles in under fifteen minutes and workout for hours at a time. Now, I cannot run for nearly as far or as long as that anymore before my body shuts it down. The humidity here doesn't help much besides sweating your body weight when you are done. It is suffocating, and I do not know how anyone can run in this type of weather. I appreciate those who can and respect the ones I see out here running in both the extreme heat and humid conditions. I always thought I would be one of those individuals, but that ended a few years ago, after my motorcycle accident, which impacted my lower back and right hip. Then a few years ago, my left foot began hurting. It started in my big toe with a pain I had not ever felt before. I basically could barely walk for a few weeks before it went away. Then it started hurting in the middle of my foot, on top of the bone above the arch. I have had to moderate how I run these days. I run on the side of my left foot now, which I am finally used to. Felt unnatural at first, and I knew it would since I have always been a front of the foot runner. I still get what I need to done. If I am on a treadmill it doesn't bother me as much and the padding on there allows me to run for consecutive miles. I am fairly good for at least ten miles on there. But when I am outside, I can barely make more than five laps around the track without being out of breath and fatigued. The two laps is a little bit over a mile, so there is a drastic difference when what my body can do inside versus outside. I have had to switch up my workout routine a few times in the last ten to fifteen years. When I was dealing with panic attacks and heart issues, I was riding a bike for thirty miles a day back in 2014 through 2016 with no running at all. I finally felt comfortable enough to begin running again in 2017 and have been able to keep it in my schedule ever since. When I got sober in 2015, working out became my escape, which it has been since the Marines. It has never left me, even though I have always been an active human and making sure I was in some type of good shape. Once I got out in 2010, I became obsessed with it. Even more so after my sobriety. It helps me in every aspect and avenue in my life. Mentally, it is my therapy session. If I can suffer and put my body through the ringer for hours at a time, it helps alleviate some of what I struggle with on a daily basis. Plus, it just feels fucking amazing to be in shape and living your life as healthy as you can. Your body is the only one you will get, obvious I know, but I remember reading about that when I was young and never really thinking much about it because of how much I hated who I was and how broken I felt. I abused this body for so long. I did not care if I lived or died to be honest with all of the shit I was dealing and struggling with in my adolescent and teen years. When I finally turned thirty years old, I could feel my body disobeying me. It hits you out of nowhere. The small pains become a larger issue if you are not careful. You become so in-tune with your mind, body, and spirit, you will do anything it takes to be as healthy as you can. That has become my life. Watching what I eat, what I do, where I go, who I give my time to. It is all imperative for the sustainability of a well rounded human. If only I had begun sooner, but I am maxing out every area of my life now without looking back. I have not even had a soda in probably twenty-five years or so. I rarely eat out, have fast food, or anything I think would be unhealthy for me. I stopped drinking milk probably twenty years ago and rarely eat bread. This book is similar to SONDER, which was basically poetry along with my own thoughts broken down into chapters. I enjoy this type of writing more, because of how I am able to just type without thinking or looking at old writings to add to pages. A true stream of consciousness is what I have been good at since I began writing.

There is not a topic off limits. I have made it a point to remain as vulnerable as I can with every single thing I do. I live my life the same way I write, openly and as transparently as possible. If others do not know who you are, you will never know who you will become if you are afraid of being judged or ridiculed. The only ones who are afraid of it, are the ones who fear everything. If you cannot take your own truth and honesty, no one will ever be able to take you seriously. I kind of went sideways with what I was getting at talking about having both of my parents still alive and spending time with my father, but that is writing for you. It takes you where you are meant to go during the process, reading or otherwise. You have to go where the energy leads you. You have to give into the immediate responses your soul feels to feel what it is your should do next. I live my life by my singular intuition alone. Not everyone has agreed with my stance in life, but I never fucking cared, because they are not the ones in charge of my life. They do not have to deal with what does or does not come from those situations. I have been fortunate and blessed with a busy mind and an endless well. If I do not drink from both, my tongue will wilt away and become some forgotten muscle that once gave me power over everything else around me. Being this way has taught me how to become more prolific in this part of my journey. I have walked countless lifetimes to arrive at this very moment in my life. I will continue to take advantage of such gifts until they no longer are appeased by how I treat them. There is no one else going to do it for you. No one else is going to guide or hold you accountable if you are not going to do it for yourself. I am appreciative of everyone who has been in my life and showed me who to be and who not to be. To this day, I am still single, never been married, and have no children. All three circumstances have been by choice, but love is a mercurial thing. Something we believe in to have power over or a hand in when it comes time for it. It will never be a choice for us. The only thing we know about it, is when it finds us, that is how it was supposed to work out all along. I took the last few days off from writing in here, but today is Monday and the sun is still burning outside of my window. The grass is all but dead, and everyone that isn't out working in this climate, are all inside. My mind is a well that never goes dry or empty. I have tried several times over the years to type, write, or even jot down things to the point of mental exhaustion and fatigue. It doesn't work that way for me. I could if I had youth on my side, write for days on end with no sleep. Some days, I feel so much I still get panic attacks, though they are not as heavy as they once were. They are at least not as bad as a decade ago, thank goodness. I focus on my breathing and know it will be okay. I read something about anxiety a few years ago, that if you stay focused on tangible objects and find something real to touch, your brain will rewire itself during any episode you may have. Even with the knowledge I have from what has been learned over the years, they still creep in and next to me when I least expect it. It is not a flaw of mine, but a truth I openly speak about.

Chapter 4

-Poetry/Prose-

Forged & Formidable

every night, i look to the moon to say thank you for bringing me a soul from the images of my dreams. the moon knows me like that, and i guess she knew you before i had kissed you that night. here's to us, as we both try to learn life as a whole. our dreams invented this place. we owe it to ourselves to live and love as if it will never become a broken reality. we are connected beyond the red string and alignment we once thought our lives to be. i am nothing more than a body of water who lost its heart to the cause, which turned me into a wilderness of shadow and fallen debris. i am still a fondly forged and undefined spectator of a human, who is searching for himself between the tranquility and hush of dusk and dawn.

Apartment Thoughts

we want life so badly, we end up selling everything inside ourselves to get it. all that is left, are the skeletons and jargon no one understands. we bleed ourselves dry for the sake of having things we won't be able to use even a few years from now. learn who you are first before jumping off mountains, hoping the clouds feel as soft as they look. there is no such thing as a cotton-candy landing when dealing with devils and monsters who are all after what it is we have and everything they lack.

Bearers

there is a certain kind of grace placed and born on the flesh of a woman who gives golden kisses to the moon without asking anything in return. you have always been more than your wings, dear one. you remain a woman of reverie and silk, all constructed by the artists that came before you. some of us create using what we know and others create by what happens or has happened to them. however you find your release, never bend the knee to anyone who has never bleed or been scarred by this life. you owe it to those who sacrificed before you in order to give you a chance for this day to become the greatest version of who they fought and died to protect. we are the bearers of life and death.

Open Invitation

i know you have been through it all over
the course of your life, the nightmares,
heartbreaks, days with no peace or sanity to
calm and ease your nerves and mind. you are
not alone in thought, mourning, grieving, or in
any movement made when space cannot be
found. i am right there with you, living it all by
your side. all you have to do is brave the
silence you fear will come next if you talk
to me about your struggles. my openness has
always been an open invitation for what you
hold back from me for your own reasons.

Hotel Enlightenment

i am opening up my scars to finally give them air to breathe. i feel love within their healing. each one that is brought to life, speaks your name. they sing your love in earthly tones and say your sweetly made whispers with the most comforting of words. "it's you. it's you. it's always been you." i am finding my way how to ultimately become my healing. i am still imagining your hands and how they showed me to love what i was, to show me the adoration it took to love all of my blurry wounds. there is no replacing a soul to soul encounter once the humans leave the room.

Back When I Knew You Better

i loved you so much, i forgot how to love anything else. there is nothing left of mine here inside this body, but it all once belonged to you. i kept it as safe as i could, and guarded it with my entire life before rearranging it to fit all of the items i had found along my way at every thrift shop, road-side, and small town cafe. my coffee is stronger these days, as is my stubbornness when it comes to moving on from anything i have touched, and in return, has touched me. i know the sun still walks beside you, just as the moon calls you back in after being out too late with your past. you have never enjoyed being told what to do. you have never loved someone telling you, no. it is why you still live your life half-alone and half in-love with everything else. you are only quiet around those whose energies do not match yours. one of the reasons we got along so well was because of our way of being the opposite personality for one another. you filled in the sky for me and i filled in the graves for you. i know you are better off than you were today, but sometimes, it is nice to think about how a heart stopped breaking.

For The Name Of Love

the night barely knows me anymore. we had been close for more than half of my life. it still loves me and owes me nothing, but it gives me the moon each night, even as the clouds get in the way, blanketing what shine is left. how fucking marvelous is that? to have a love so deep and true that it gives me its best effort to show me love still matters. that love is the epicenter for all humans to be born again in the name of light and sweet lullabies.

Where The Lonely Go

prop me up against the grave and litter the ground with millions of petals. maybe then you will see where the lonely go when there is no space left for their ache in this world. maybe then a name will mean something to you and a face will become more humanly to you.

Time and All It Destroys

we all hope for a brighter day, more infinite shimmer, less and less fracturing and fraying. a more thought of and balanced approach to the depths of light and dark cavities of our story. survivors, we are, and always will be. one day, i will find words that matter to someone, and in return, i will have the greatest story ever told, spoken, and written about. i will have that particular someone who becomes the true integrity of every single word, instead of merely being an unaccompanied time-stamp, waiting on the clock to punch out and go home to nothing again to remember what was lost.

Safely, Homely, Inwardly

i will always love the momentary pauses this universe gives me to think of you. i will keep safe the moments of when they remind me of you, either by license plates, your football team, tv shows, and movies we once watched together through our phone screens. every one of our songs and the ones you told me to listen to because you thought i would like them, still have their own playlist. all the way to how someone uses a curse word as you once did when that was all the patience you had left. any and everything in my life these days, returns you back to me, safely, homely, and inwardly. a true measure of what love means.

Five Thousand Reasons Never To Again

i will never forget the time when she threw her engagement ring onto the pavement. it was out of nowhere and right after eating out with our friends. i had spent over five thousand dollars on it, after picking it out the night before i picked her up at the airport. it was the only purchase i made from the money i made while fighting in Afghanistan. i told her the night we left North Carolina i would marry her. the only thing i thought about while i was overseas, was getting back to her to do just that. when she threw it, i knew our life together was over. the diamond was not scratched and the ring itself did not break, but my heart shattered into million fucking pieces. i would eventually find the aftermath of it all over the East Coast, from North Carolina, South Carolina, and parts of Virginia. it would be the last time i ever thought about marriage, about ever giving power to someone else through monetary value that they could break again after almost dying to get back to them. love is fragile enough without adding onto it with a material item that can be tossed away.

Fostered

kiss me underneath the light. i want to see the moon in you. i want to see how it becomes an image i will never forget. i want to live anywhere inside of it, inside of you. kiss me, and take me away from this earth. i have been here too long without you, without a reason to move forward in whatever space this is called now. i am all yours, in all the ways i once belonged to the darkness i was fostered by.

Horizontally

for all of the things life has taken away and given to me, i am soulfully and wholly thankful that you happened to me. i would not have been able to know who i was or how to intimately love someone else who gave their partner significance and refuge for the lonely invading their lands. someone who knew how to hold my face without breaking the porcelain i had been made from. broken and displaced, i had lived a life of delicacy and fragility before you taught me how beautiful it is to break for the things we love in a manner of immediate relief and sanctuary. i was nothing until you took your body and placed it next to mine, horizontally.

Life's Chain Reaction

i am blessed to feel it all, light, love, and the incurable ache. some things you must fucking feel engrossed by, with purpose and occurrence, to know if it is for you. if it is, make a dwelling out of it. make love to it. write about it. talk about it. listen to it with comprehension. it will be with you until it speaks its last words, and i hope you believe in it enough for a true change to detonate inside of you, causing the chain reaction this entire world needs to be a part of. a pure line of fire, we will become.
all without ashes or worries left behind.

In the Becoming

i was made to be a constant wanderer. it only makes sense now because my soul loves to remain on the outside of life, on the outside of this human i have become in search of things meant to make my fucking soul dance and gravitate towards in the pursuit of a lively face to show for it at the end of it all.

Immortal Things

i am everlastingly and profusely going to grow old with you, in distance or embrace, i will. there will never come a time when i am not calling out to you, running to you, or making sure the moon is where she is supposed to be for you at all times. you are someone who should never know what waiting feels like, what being left entirely alone with your own thoughts can do to a preciousness like you. your worries are mine, just as the sky lights up whenever we talk about what it is we are after. there is a connection beyond the grave itself between you and i. one that could never keep either of us six feet down or scattered like ash, kissing breezes and birds that find what remains from a love born from immortal things.

Worth The Suffering

i did not know i would have to get over this feeling again. this emptiness. this fucking pain. it eats at me more than most. it is my biggest fear of life. being left by someone who said they would ever leave. i thought the last time would be it for me. but now, i have to learn how to go through it all over to find meaning and purpose. you say you are still here, but you are not. the only thing that remains of you are the words you never told me that i am now writing to get out of me. may there always be meaning found within this suffering.

Beyond The Orange And Red

love never taught me how to be normal. i may never find the perfect or pristine time for what i am looking for. others seem to be content, not looking, or wanting what i want. that is life though, finding stable and common ground in an uncommon reality where tender love is nothing more than missing everything all at once. where life meets death for the first time, and you realize how it is all connected to a larger plan at hand. something beyond the orange and red outlined by a sun and blood spilled to fill your mouth and heart again and again for years and lifetimes ahead of where you are now. may it be worth your life.

What Are You Here For

there are too many self-help gurus and life quotes out here done by those whom have never lived a single day their entire lives. it saddens me how so many take their word as to how to live and love. if you come to my page and you feel differently after reading anything i write, i am doing my job, my part in this hectic landscape. i am not here for the recycled jargon this environment has become. i am here to be an escape from the everyday life.

Nothing Spared

to be missed, is to be loved, and what a sightly feeling it is to have it be real. the love may never be enough for some of us, but to those whom wish for nothing else, i hope it arrives altogether and thoroughly. i can only hope we all know how it feels to be missed lovingly, without anything being spared to save for later, with absolutely no flesh left on the bones.

Words You May Never Hear Again

i get consumed by you easily throughout my day. i awake, and if you are not the first single thought i have, you are not far behind my first cup of coffee. i am all about you more than i tell you about. i needed you to know that. i am forever grateful for this way of feeling with you. i will continuously love and adore the sensitivity you use on me, as if you had known all along how long i had been without it. i need your human, your honest, all of your directed breaths. i will bring you coffee and sit with you at the table or in bed when you feel as though your body needs an extra five minutes of rest you once told me about when i first spoke to you. i will gladly sip my coffee and stare into your infinity without hesitation or looking away at what other beauty you have created for me to see. your nakedness is what i will lay with when you need my hands and body to lead you somewhere else.

Territorial

i wear her fingerprints as if they are the most expensive item i own. i wear her marks proudly. she has pronounced her territory, and i am hers. whenever the moon howls, i am left in awe, as she transforms into the goddess i need. every night her beautiful screams bring me to life. the only thing she loved more than me, were the stars. the reason being was when i was out of breath to say her name, they made up for the moans i could not get out. they called out to her every time we came upon a wish we could not taste ourselves. I will devour you in this life, and whatever finds us across the rooms we find ourselves in, naked or clothes in fiery pursuit.

A Promise Made

it was not a resolution. it was a promise to myself. i wanted to get better at everything i did, as well as healthier and stronger in my soul, mind and body. they have been weakened at times over the years, but i needed them to be herculean for me this year. i finally opened my heart to someone who cared for life as much as i did. though she is not mine yet in this life, i know in the next realm we could last until the sun burns out and the moon falls slowly to her own death. when all aspects of life and beyond have been met and found, with all smiles, we will gather ourselves softly, then return to where it all began for us.

Where Soul Touches Bone

beauty speaks and the devil bends at the knee to welcome in a unique mystique of mystery and grace. i have seen flames that could overtake an entire ocean in the eyes of a dreamer who never knew how to give up what they loved. it is all about the redefined glory, the redesign of holy matrimony that takes us to the brink of war between ourselves. we are the artists never satisfied with a finished product, which is why we tend to destroy everything upon its completion. the ending seems monotonous, a tiresome act of dying and coming back to life in the same breath. i have been hypersensitive since a young age. i knew a difference was merely me disagreeing with anyone who had something different to tell me when i had already made up my mind. fascinated by colors and movement, i began writing out everything i could not move my mouth to convey. writing became my language, a barrier between those who wanted to be close to who i was. it felt as though i was keeping everyone a continent away based on being unable and unequipped to compartmentalize my own deepening struggles with being a soul living in a controlled human environment. i live purposely underneath the current, taking my cues from a subterranean point of view. the darkness did not choose me. i chose everything inside of it, because it felt safe to be alone with something that did not judge me for not knowing what i wanted to become in this winding and twisting existence. being different has become the ultimate ally. my vulnerability is infinitely sized in its demeanor. i rarely say a single fucking word if i do not find a common bond, a single thread of connection within the first few minutes of meeting. i have been seated with love next to me, holding onto a part of hope that i would finally say something in return. i wish i was next to you. if i were, i would never go back to blue, to feeling as if i was not good enough to know a drop of truth felt in a monsoon. i believe if you find truth being spoken in a crowded room, it will give birth to a new idea to believe in. i want you to see me as i see myself now. i want you to view me as someone who found his way back to himself by killing off every version that tried to kill him first. i am decorated in a scarring display of humanity, but i would not mind your eyes on me. i do not pray anymore. i have not spoken to god in over a decade. the spirits keep me company. the energy feeds me out here. the walks with my dad and brother are my religion. sundays were made for confessions to be between soul and stone out here, between birds and nature. an infinite exists wherever your feet meet the land. the free are those who were bound by a brokenness only scars can provide. out here, we all come from them. we all know the path before our feet ever speak of its name to us and lead the way.

<u>On The Outskirts</u>

most days, i sit behind the wind and watch it blindly escape the mundane stretched out over the yawn of every mountain attempting to blend in. other days, i sit reluctantly in front of this typewriter, writing about anything i can in order to forget about a past i cannot forget. i am wearing a borrowed smile, a hoodie from London, and dirt on my bones from the last time i had to dig myself out of the hole i died inside to bring parts of your love back to life. my happiness is not spoken about, but i seem to shy away from asking myself honest questions, because the truth is terrifying when you are not ready to hear the answers you are hiding from. i am over you, sounds a hell of a lot better than, i am getting better, i am almost there.

Chapter 5

-Stories-

Today is Tuesday, and the heat is still unbearable. We had the hottest day yet a few days ago. 115 degree heat index. It will be like this the remaining of the month. Texas does not have four seasons in progression like most states. We are lucky to have two or three a year, but sometimes, we get all four in one. We have not had any rain in over a month. The grass is dormant just as it was last year. You wake up, and by the time eight thirty rolls around, it is already over one hundred degrees. My life is nothing as I thought it would be by now. I never had plans for marrying after the age of twenty-four. I never wanted kids after that age either, so when I say I am not where I thought I would be, it means physically where I am at. I knew I would always have the caretaker side of me. I knew I would always be able to help anyone I was with and provide for them should they need it. I feel as though I am running a nursing home here with my father. He can still do things and remains active, but with me being the only one driving now and who has a vehicle, I feel as though I have more pressure tied to every limb of mine.

I cannot go anywhere, because if I were to leave for an extended amount of time, it would mean me leaving my father here without any means or something to drive. My frustration has nothing to do with him, though I do wish he would just move out of this fucking house. I do not see that happening for whatever reason. This groundhog day routine is killing me. I can feel the suffocation each morning I wake up and each night I go to bed. I know what my day will be like before it ever happens. I do not function that way. Yes, I like certain routines and ways of life, but doing the same shit over and over and over again will kill anyone, or at least weaken their spirit. The energy in this house is beginning to resemble the kind that my mother's house has, heavy, dark, and constantly shifting moods. I love my father to death, but it isn't sustainable living here, especially when I am the only one working. I would not mind getting a second job just to have extra cash to take care of certain things, but then again, it would mean my father being without a vehicle if something were to happen or if he needed to go do something. We are halfway through August now, the dog days remain barking and howling. I can still remember the day Kobe Bryant died which seems like yesterday, but ever since the pandemic, this world has felt more like a simulation than real life. Everything is incredibly more expensive now. You cannot go to the grocery store and spend less than fifty to seventy-five dollars for two bags of items. Whenever we go into town for groceries, we usually get three to four bags worth. It is insane what you can and cannot afford these days. Eggs were once over seven dollars a carton. Now, they are back below two dollars and fifty cents. Oatmeal is over five dollars now. Anything remotely or close being healthy is something you can forget about walking out of there with anything left for gas to fuel up for the week. As of today, price for gas is three dollars and twenty-nine cents. Down from what it was this time last week, when it was almost thirty cents higher. This life is not for the middle or lower third class of America anymore. If you are not constantly making a source of income, it will eat you up without hesitation and not even have the decency to spit you back out. I feel for any family trying to survive these days. My older brother has three kids. All under the age of twelve. He is the only one working right now and has all kinds of debt, but he is making it work. I go to the store and see a few families with half a cart full of items, hoping it will last the full week. I can see the pain on their faces, knowing it will not be enough, but their children seem to be happy and carefree which is a blessing during these times we are living in. Making the most of it is all any of us can do. We must remember that it is only temporary. Anything and everything we do and think of remains temporary in this world and on this journey. I remind myself daily to live this life one day at a time, one breath at a time, one step at a time. Anything more than that, and my anxiety can cripple me to the point of walking out of the door becoming a checklist item for me to mark down. One small victory for me goes a long way when you suffer from mental disorders. But I have never allowed it to truly define who I am. Instead, I use it as fuel and motivation throughout my day. I use it to write clearer, with a more vivid sense of articulating what it is I am actually trying to say on days when nothing feels good coming out of my mouth. Some days, it is too blurry to make out what the message is, but I do my best to decipher what my soul is trying to relay to me. To live is to suffer. It is up to us how much and to what extent we do. It is up to us to see how much we can tolerate during a daily basis when we are a few moments away from giving up for the day. In order for you to know who it is you are, you must break away from the comforts you are familiar with. You must understand your emotions and why they impact you the way you do. One particular thing I carry with me is grief. I have never really defined what it is for me, because it has been with me my entire life. The death, the loss, the absence, anything resembling what once was, it all is within me. It is something I write about daily so I can see how far I have come and how much I have grown despite it raging inside of me. My life is based upon it. It is the only thing that truly knows me and treats me with a certain love and respect, because I treat it the same way. I can write about it, cry about it, and scream with it right alongside me, but if I do not interact with it, it doesn't change and neither do I. I have experienced too much life for it to not have changed me in some way. I know for certain I am not the same person I was yesterday or last month or a few moments ago. I am an ocean's wave in those regards, constantly moving and evolving into something bigger, smaller, infinite. It has been such a beautiful journey, and I look forward to the rest of it for however long this planet will have me and for as long as I still add meaning and value to this path. In the past four or five years, all that has happened, is change. Be it to us or what is and is not around us anymore. A delicate fate takes place between the dusk and dawn. Upon waking, I already know what kind of a day it will be for me and those around me. I have said before that I am a walking nerve, exposed to feel and react the way I need to, so I can make the best decisions for myself. Being here has dampened and darkened my path a bit, but I have not allowed it or given it power to destroy who I am or what I do. It is crucial to stay as focused as we can on the task at hand. I know it will not always be this way. I know change is inevitable and the only thing constant in this lifetime. We all get the same twenty-four hours. It has always been a choice as to what we do with it all. Some of us do not even get that, which should add even more determination to your own life to maximize anything you do. I know tomorrow morning when I get up at seven, I will have my coffee, watch about thirty minutes of Get Up, set out my workout clothes, and be on the track before eight thirty. I know it will be over one hundred degrees out there. I know I will need to go to the post office and run whatever other errands I need to. I know all of this and how it has been this exact routine for a few months, ever since I broke my treadmill. I still get up thankful because my father is sitting in his recliner with the TV paused, waiting on me to sit down to watch it. I am grateful, because he is still here to enjoy the routine he has made for himself. For some of us, that is all we have to live for and all we have to look forward to. Life does not wait on anyone. It happens with or without your consent. The sooner you realize how this life works, the sooner you will understand how you should and should not spend your time here. I have pages full of things I would love to do now and places to go, but I cannot, because of my father. It is not his fault he lost his job, but I do wish he would have been more frugal with his money and what he spent it on while he had more than enough to retire comfortably. Now, he barely has enough to pay rent and get himself food. He is down to one hundred and eighty-five pounds. I could not be more proud of him. He has lost around thirty to forty pounds since last year with him walking and eating healthier because of what I am able to get and make for him. One of the hardest things in life is watching your parent(s) grow old. You never really see it growing up because you are too busy constantly doing the exact same thing. But once life is able to catch up with you and you are given a few months to pause and take in what is happening, you come to an abrupt stop with where you are and where your parents are. My father still has a full head of hair, but you can see it starting to lose its hold ever so slightly. It is almost enough to make you break down in front of them if you are not careful about it. He takes more naps now and by the time night-time arrives, he has already slept half of it away. I honestly do all I can to preserve time as much as possible when I am done with my work and settled in for the night. In 2021, he almost died due to having pneumonia and Covid. I took him to three different hospitals before finding one that would take him in and give him the proper treatment. I remember when I got back from Red Rocks and seeing him not improve at all the first two weeks of my return. I would go to bed after him, get up a few times to stand in front of his door and listen to make sure he was still breathing. It has scarred me for the rest of my time here without question. I find myself always checking to see if his chest is rising when he is taking his naps. I always tend to stand at the end of my hallway to make sure I hear him snoring or talking in his sleep to know I can go to bed and not worry about him that night. It is the little things in life that stay with you and haunt you for the rest of time. They are the reminders of why we are living and what we are living for. I hope one day down the road, I can actually get back out in the real world. I miss it dearly. I miss being around other creatives and people like me. I wrote something a few weeks ago about me wanting to change the way prose and poetry were written, read and thought about. I want to change the entire landscape of it and bring in a newer generation who believes in living and what it stands for. I want to explore all areas of it and bend it and twist it into something this world has never seen before. Being here challenges that aspect for me, but it will not hinder or stop me from making it happen. To be able to write for a living like I do now is the biggest blessing there is. Not everyone gets to do what they love and less than that ever find something they truly love doing. I am not one to settle just because I have to. I will never conform to the societal views others have or tend to have. I am not the machine or cog in the wheel that will keep that engine going. If you are not trying to break free from such things, we are not the same, and I do not wish to ever be around such humans or energy. Forward motion always, in all ways. For us to find ourselves and who we are meant to be, it will take a different version for each week, month, and year we are given. We are all asked to be something for someone else, but if you wish to become someone beyond the thoughts in your own head, you will need to put action behind your speech. You will need to be able to sacrifice things you once thought you could never live without to get to that certain place of security and freedom of being the human you need. Today is Thursday, and another day that isn't asking a lot out of me that I have not already poured out and into today. I am nearing a balance in my life I have long sought-after. No girlfriend yet for me, and I say, yet, because I truly believe once it is meant to take place, it will. I believe what has fucked me up the most is always trying to fill that fucking void with someone I was not ready for, with someone I was forcing myself to not necessarily love, but allow in my space. Each relationship I have been in, it has been warranted to some degree. Each one has failed, even if I did not want it to. It has been over two years now since the last time I had someone to talk to, hold, and sleep with in the same bed. Those little aspects of life and love go unnoticed while it is all happening and taking place. We take so much for granted because deep down we believe all we have is all we will ever need. I believe fate and destiny play a large role in our lives. I had a conversation today with someone about that exact thing. They were telling me they do not believe in it as much as I do, because their scientific side would not allow them to. I live my life by intuition and feel. I live my life by breaking patterns and giving myself the best opportunity to seize every ounce of light from the sky. I am odd, different, a bit over-the-top when it comes to daily things. I always seem to be looking for something beyond what that something means for me and for someone else. I do not dissect things more than I need to, nor do they need to have a reason for finding me the way they do. I simply charge life with full strides and a soul that will not allow me to settle for anything other than what it knows I need. That is why love to me has always been the pinnacle of life. It is why I look for it in everything I do and whatever passes me on the street or in my field of view. I went to the grocery store today and as I was checking out and leaving. The woman by the doors told me, "have a great day," with a shy smile and then looked away. I have people all the time telling me to have a good day and things of that nature, but when someone says something you are not expecting, it feels all the better to your heart and allows you to breathe a bit slower knowing they are taking time to share a sentiment with you. A few minutes later, I walked by a Harley Davidson with a custom OD Marine paint-job. It was missing decals and seemed to be super basic besides the color. I told myself it was not owned by a military person, vet, or anything related to those things. It was trying to be too much of one thing, especially being a generic bike to belong to anyone besides a human of the same cloth. The guy that owned it, was putting on his helmet and getting ready to start it. I said, "nice bike." He did not even look at me or acknowledge what I had said. Just as I was about to get into my car and start the engine, he said, "Oh, thanks." He was just some wannabe biker wearing newly bought jeans, cowboy boots, no tattoos, and some brand-name button down T-shirt. You can always tell who others are by feel or gut instincts. Vibes never lie and I knew he was an asshole who bought the bike, got it painted a certain color that would reflect a military lifestyle he was not a part of. He did not even own a cut, so it was just another sign for us to always be on the lookout for anyone attempting to impose themselves on a world that is ninety-nine percent facade to fit in with the rest of the crowd who looks forward and does not think about what they are doing or why they are doing it. They do it because they saw it in a movie or read about it in some book to make themselves feel better about their own lives. More power to them I guess, but that is not my lifestyle and not for me. I was raised around a bike when my dad got his first Harley. I still remember vividly when he brought it home and unloading it out of the trailer. I got on the back of it and I was hooked. I knew then I would one day want to own one. I finally did several years ago after passing my driving test and not really ever riding one as most of the guys did at the course that day. I was never comfortable on it, but I wanted to prove to myself I could. I did not have anyone around when I was growing up to teach me how to drive stick-shift. Another thing I have never been comfortable doing. My mind does not work that way and I could never comprehend clutch, gas, break, and using them all at the same time. Somehow, I was able to make the motorcycle thing work, but it did not end well for me. I was riding it around the park roads where we lived in 2015 and someone pulled out in front of me while I was making a corner. I had two choices, run off into the ditch and hit a guardrail or lay it down on the asphalt road. I chose the latter and flew over my handle bars and landed directly on my back. The bike nearly crushed me as soon as I hit the pavement, but it missed. I ended up fucking my back and hip fairly substantial, but never actually went to get my injuries checked out by a doctor.

I suffered for a few months before it felt as though I was healed and aligned again. I still deal with chronic back and hip pains, as if my body needed more abuse. I took the corner going the speed limit, which was thirty-five miles an hour, but when I was launched from the bike, I was doing well over forty-five or fifty. I picked the bike up and rode it back to the house. It ended up costing me fifteen hundred dollars to get the damage fixed on the bike and it was the last time I rode it. It was finally sold a few years ago. I will never ride again. When I was in rehab back in 2009, I met a guy in there who was training at Annapolis. He told some of us his story and why he was in there. He mentioned he almost died on a bike going well over seventy miles an hour on the highway. He laid it down and slid his way into a guardrail. Thankfully he was not seriously injured and I do not know how he survived. I had heard stories like that my entire life. It never deterred me from wanting to ride one day. I remember vividly the first time I saw someone riding a bike. It was on the movie, Top Gun. If you know the movie, you remember Tom Cruise riding his Ninja by the airport and racing the jets that were taking off. It was one of the most impactful things I remember as a kid and it stuck with me and still sticks with me today. But as I said previously, I will never get on one again. I value my life a lot more these days and there are a million different ways that you can kill yourself while seeking an adrenaline rush. I find myself not being more fearful these days, but abundantly more cautious with what I am doing and want to do. I was never that way before in my life. I was always all in, balls out, seeking some sort of adventure. My anxiety has caused me to become a different person, or maybe it is just me maturing into someone who realizes he does not need to take unnecessary risks anymore. I find joy in the moments when I am out in a national park, with my brothers and father, or taking a road-trip. I am content with my happiness being the furthest thing away of what it once was and meant to me. Maybe I am boring to a lot of people, but I know what does and does not make me happy. At the end of the day that is all we can ask and hope for. I know many who are relentless when it comes to finding something, anything that makes their heart full. I could watch College Football all day on a Saturday and go to bed with the biggest smile on my face. I could also randomly decide to take a road-trip to Arizona or Utah and be as full as anyone else. It all comes down to what we are comfortable with in the older parts of our journey. Change is the constant we look for. If it is not that way for you, you will never grow as a human. Being who I am today, it has made me stop and think about a lot of what I have done with my life. It has given me pause to reflect on the decisions I have made and never fucking cared to make. I could have died fifty times by now, and I will take that as a sign that my life still matters. I still feel as though my purpose has yet to be complete, and that is my driving force to this day. Writing as openly as I do, I hope it connects to someone who is going through their own struggles, some sort of rock bottom, and shines a light for them to use on their own path. It took me the longest time to acknowledge my failures were for me to use.

Chapter 6

-Poetry/Prose-

Infinity And Her Shadows

drugs, alcohol, and self-inflicted wounds take so many of us too soon. do not be afraid to say what is on your mind. no one is more important than the next. we are enough. i'm not sure what love is anymore. is it a true feeling? is it just a word? is it more than anything or anyone can describe? i know it exists. i have felt it before, but these nights when i look up at the ceiling, my intuition works in ways at times i don't understand or comprehend. but that has never been the case when it came to you. it feels your every move, fully awake and visibly alive in my dreams. i look to my sky and see no moon. i do not see you anywhere around me anymore. this life of mine is a darkened path filled with never-ending and inescapable twists and turns. when you leave me for only a single second, my anxious hands search frantically, feeling the sharp edges of the blinding shadows. i swear an infinity has come and gone. i am in constant search of you, and that will never change.

Case Of The Mondays

one of the many reasons i write is to release the demons i've harbored inside of me. i wish you could have seen just how i allowed them to use my bruised and bloody heart as a punching bag and my soul as a blanket to cover up with during the four seasons of winter i had been forced to freeze in. i use the words as a heating source now. warming every inch of what they tried to kill. you might be able to think that you can fucking use and abuse me at times, but i fucking swear to the gods, i will always end up fighting my way out of the blistering cold and hopeless nights. if i cannot love you as is, then i will learn to love you as a friend. i'd rather have you that way, then not have you at all. it took me years to arrive at that conclusion, but it has been worth it because you matter more to me than anyone ever has before. to live this life without you in any capacity, would mean decapitating my soul and stretching what is left of me from one side of the country all the way to the other, causing me to rip and dry out from the baking sun and winter's breath.

Caution Tape and B-Sides

i used to fucking hate you. now, i know why you are the first day of every month. it is a time to prepare and reflect on everything you have done. a place when time seems to drag by as if all of the hands in the world are holding onto the second, trying to keep it from moving. over the years, i have learned to appreciate you more and value the time we spent in the vast spaces of my mind, remembering all of the times before when i was a teenager when it felt like clocks did not exist, because i never knew how to appreciate time. sometimes, i think if words were money, you would've tried harder and actually stayed. i enjoy sitting in the silence. it is only then can i hear the words you meant to say to me, "i cannot promise you i will stay." you had made up your mind months before, but i could never quite see beyond the pillars of my own emotions. you left like the last breath exhaled by anxiety as it finally lost the battle. maybe one day i will be able to find something worth salvaging, something entirely new and replaced for someone else to hold onto. there is no moon in my sky tonight. i guess the universe knew i needed to be alone for a while after you left. it's when all else fails that we truly learn how to hold on completely. as we go through life, we experience everything as one, and together, we witness a growth of longevity in our hearts, because we knew what others had failed to understand about losing something turning into a blessing in disguise. we live by the creed of believing we have all the answers based purely on having lived through such things. we become entirely bent around our own thoughts and have no way of coming away from them. growing up, there will always be those people constantly forcing words and thoughts into your mind. they will try and deceive you into thinking they, too, know it all, and better than you because they have a more pronounced scar running down the left side of their chest where they had something someone else wanted more than they did. be careful with your pauses and who you take a break from life for. be cautious of any human looking as if they have it all figured out. they will be the first one to come after your love.

In The Backseat

i know nothing, but i have been in love a few times before. i guess that makes me someone who thinks they know more about it than the one who has yet to break. truth is, no one ever will understand why we fall in and out of it. some people go into it wanting a specific thing, while others gather it all up and hold onto it, hoping it doesn't go anywhere. what once was a turn on, now makes us cringe in bodies who cannot stand being near the person we once could never live without. whether it is time, expired feelings, or simply us checking out and changing who we are, love will always come and go like summer being fucked by fall in the backseat of our first car. our evolution lives and dies within those changes.

Waiting In Line

i do not know if i will ever find someone or if i will die alone. i am not sure people who are my age give that any or much thought at all, but i do. i wonder every fucking second about things, about life, about my next step. it all matters to me. it is all about consistency with who you are. when it is time, what you want and need will present itself to you. you will have to decide if you are ready for it or if it is needed. of all the billions of people in this world, it is hard to fathom how many true connections there are and could potentially be when we are all connected to someone and everyone at the same time. you will not meet them all though. could you imagine standing in line, waiting to meet every human there is? i do, and i would wait a lifetime to have that opportunity, to have that mirrored feeling.

Where The Soul Goes

i see the sun, and it is how my energy becomes potent. it is how my brittle heart syncs with the universe. it is how i can make my vivid dreams more visible, tangible, realistic. it is how a gasp becomes a breath, and makes it easier to take and give away. it is how these toffee bones in me become fortified and equipped well enough to take on the marvelous mountains when they once tried to break me in-half to use them for their own posturing ways. some humans would tell you, the higher the peak, the bigger of lie. those same humans would tell you, the further the climb is, the weaker it will ultimately make you in the end. for those who believe that nonsense to be true, they obviously have never been in love with the escape they provide. up there, you eventually become no one. up there, you find spirituality to be alone in silence and peace. to be close enough to talk to the gods, makes the trip back down all the more reason to understand we are nothing more than a human living a soul's life and journey.

Announced

there will be days beyond this one that are brighter, more full, and more wholesome than anything you have ever been a part of in your life. these particular days may feel extremely far away and in-between, but they exist. i can only hope your eyes hold them a bit longer. never forget your powers and who you are. you are an entire ocean, living and breathing, as the waves call you mother, father, friend, lover, whomever they need you to be for them during that specific time and day.

First And Last Time

i feel your petite breath, all warm and subtle, right next to my tepid cheek. i look directly at you, your eyes closed, asleep and at rest. if love is to be anything, allow it to be this, with you, with us, with this very precise and sentimental moment of knowing exactly what you feel like next to me. my steady eyes and attention will never leave you, not even for the moon or any other cosmic creature. if this becomes our life, may death take us both by the hand at the same time. i would gladly walk through infinities of darkness to discover you all over again, naked, vulnerable, and waiting for me to touch you for the first time, for the last time.

TEACHER

i realized a few years later, i was not worthless after all. when love left me, i knew what was coming next would be worth more than the love she could not give me back in return. i hope you find someone who sees you and knows they will never have to look for anyone else for the rest of time. the one in a million faces that makes you feel as if you belong to this planet finally. to find someone like that, brings all your pieces together in a way no one could ever before. it is all about the effort we show and give ourselves that teaches someone else how to treat us. be kind to your human side. we are all fighting things no one else can see until you open up to them. if you are to trust anything, trust in the fact that the only way things get worse, is by allowing them to.

The Places We Go

i need you to know there is still fire in my blood for you. days may become thoughtless for others in this withering place, but not me, not with you. i have collected every deep red rose for you, every sand dollar from Florida to California. with you, it has never just been about the moments or the nights when stars sat in awe of your truth. it has been about my need for you. my purpose for loving you is about never forgetting you in all lifetimes.

Interstellar

you come to me often, as a dream, as a thought dressed in an outfit you once bought while we were together. there are certain days when i feel nothing except everything from you. your kisses, your eyes, and missing what you were to me, it all finds me when i least expect it. you were the softest thought for me. it never took me overthinking to know you were too good for me or if i was too good to you. i have been in the fire since you left, all ashes and mourning now. but being a fighter, you learn how to keep swinging until there are no more punches worth being thrown. this empty space, this infinite void you left for me, is now mine to defend. may life bend and sway with me, as it moves further away from your memory.

HOMELESS

and i said, come down, won't you stay here a while, just one more kiss, one more holding, one more momentary reflection of your flesh upon my own. you told me you couldn't stay any longer, but i could not let you go back up there to lean back into the darkness without me. to be the moon, you must remain alone, i understand. here i am, floating and fighting off waves, knowing how much needing you kills me all the same. being without you brings me back to the same place you found in me all those years ago, three feet from a bottomless grave. you are the light my blood runs to, the pirouette my body twists and turns for. i will walk this world as i have before, a soul with no body as a home, with nobody around to tell me, "please come back down where we need you, back where you lovingly belong."

Where The Light Goes

as the leaves begin to change, i, too, can feel a newness. i, too, am finally letting go of what i have kept alive for my own reasons. the air around me seeps into me and sweeps me into orange and brown piles. it is there in mid-leap, i crash into love once again. it is there i find my footing once again to lift myself back up with my roots demanding me to reaffirm my own beliefs, truths, and sense of direction. if i am to be anyone, i will search relentlessly for my own spot where the shade i put off does not keep all of the light within me fro touching.

UNIFICATION

between the small talk and hand gestures, lives were changed by throwing away the sun before words became expressions based on a lifelong pursuit of change. drinking made it easier to live, to get by, to forget about the child who was left behind. drinking made it easier to die, a quiet attempt to love myself in a thousand empty rooms. sobriety taught me patience, a held pause between human and mirror. sobriety taught me how to live proudly, an entourage of encouragement no longer based on illusions perceived to be forsaken. my lessons are mine alone. i bare these bones and speak openly about my failures, because without them, i would still be drinking alone, thinking i was the only one with a past that needed to be killed off along with its host. we found each other during a season of bruising, a coldness so bitterly abusing, we almost did not go through with meeting one another. we hung up the phone every time with our laughter being the last thing we heard. your beauty taught me how love seeps into those who believe themselves to be worthless, but discover a secret kept by a breathless decree of salvation. reinvigorate me, unconditionally and freely. reinvent me, quietly and lovingly. i am done self-loathing. i am done ruining myself for the sake of starting over. i am me, because of you, because of your teachings. we are sunlight dancing rambunctiously, boisterously, in unified unison.

UNEARTHING A MEMORY

life is meant to be seen though the spectrum of love. our eyes would always be fixated on each other, making damn sure our vision was always focused on the plentiful desires we both had an appetite for, life, love, trust, and the promise to always see the other as if it were the first time, every time. every dedication and word spoken and whispered between you and i, became a novel we both poured our heart and soul into. whenever i feel as if missing you could take me back behind the curtains of these eyes where all things loved and forgotten get slaughtered, i keep them open with all the courage i have left. they remain focused on what we had, on what you gave me, on all things that will have life again once the dirt gets removed from my mouth and organs.

Cosmic Oath

some nights, i stay awake as long as i can, worrying and thinking of nothing about me. all i am consumed by, is directed at others, hoping they have everything they need and wondering if people have the same comforts as me. i do not have a lot to my name these days, but i know it's more than most have right now. i will continue to try and strive for a better life, while battling through each detour this road leads me to. when i am able to hear the sweet sounds of the ocean and walk on endless fields of sand with you, i will know how it feels to have everything i once thought i could never have, a life spent sharing limitless sunrises and sunsets with someone i could only hope to grow old with, as the sun and moon die together in sweet reverie, while watching over you and i, as they go beyond the promise they carried for one another.

WONDERMENT

someone, somewhere, is wondering about you. wondering when they will be able to thank you for not giving up on what you both felt, but could never explain until now. you are how someone knows where magic comes from. you are the reason why someone still aspires to be some form of good, hoping for better to find them. inspirations are simply carved out of anger, grief, and absence. we choose who we are based on what has happened to us, and how we allow it to guide our creating hands. love is an anomaly, often referred to as a sleeping guest who only wishes to be woken up to watch the sun fall and set beyond the pines and grassy lands it is filtered by. we are never a finished product, but adoration adds shine to our bones of which we continually kill ourselves to be colored by and accepted for.

Smile Back

when i kissed you, you brought me back to life, back to the beginning where nothing hurt and i was able to go through life without pain bearing down on me. you gave the universe reason to continue creating, to keep endlessly living and loving all the space it had yet to claim within you. you will always be the first kiss shared between the sun and moon, all passion, all miracle, all light. it alone gave me this journey, this now, this ache to forever be yours however you need me. beside you or miles away, my love will only stay for the breaths you take from me in exchange for the moans you give back to me willingly. laying or standing, wherever it is you vehemently call upon something greater than what you discover, may it observe you in your harmonious state, laughing and smiling as if death was never after you to begin with.

WOMAN

there is nothing more magical in this universe than a woman with a full heart who never feels as if she needs to apologize for it. you will come across a million faces in your lifetime, if not more. once you see hers, you will know for certain why you were put into this world. you will know why poetry and art was created. you will understand without question why muses never die, but live longer than every god that once thought themselves to be immortal in the eyes of the witnesses who saw them transform suns and moons into humans. you will feel her light long before you see her smile. she is not hiding who she is from you. she is protecting the innocence still existing where the devil tried to take away what was left after her childhood left her shelter-less and scarred. there are burial grounds she will never mention, but once she allows you to hold her for the night, you will know all too well how much human she is.

The Art Of Goodbye

you were the one for me and being together was never going to happen in a reality existing now. i can dwell on it all i want, but you are getting married to him and i am divorcing you from my memories. a cleansing has taken place. i have dusted these shelves, boxed up every safely kept, i love you, swept away tears and goodbyes, and washed everything you had once touched before, including my own life. the windows are cleaned, beautifully stained with shine and new moons. i do not wish you the worst, because it has already happened to you. i only wish you find forgiveness for yourself and the fragile woman you left behind in search of someone you could never become. your crisis is nothing more than knowing what you had is better than what you have now. i feel sorry for you, truly, but it is time for the sorrow i have had since you left to be given proper rest and release for teaching me what you never learned from your own.

<u>*Somewhere In The Newness*</u>

i am in a weird phase of life. i do not expect anyone to understand, unless they have felt as though you do not want anyone or anything. all you want is space, more space, and more space. i only want to travel, to get away fully from society, from behind the screen and away from technology. i want nature to move me as the mountains i have moved, new lands, new faces, new language, new food. i am in the pursuit of newness, of anything touching my soul and accepting its light and dark with love and adoration for the survival it has been through. i am ready to meet myself in the beginning of a feeling that begins with my acceptance for what i have been through.

<u>*All The Faces Within Me*</u>

there is a feeling, a steady and holy feeling when i am around you. there are no gods asking for my name these days, but you do, you did. to be called upon by a lover, turns earth into a moveable force. an inertia of immaculate beauty moves though spaces, moves through sealed off walls, acting as a barrier for letting go. there are no gods in my life, but the gods do not know about you. whenever you speak openly, a wilderness of wolves come out to hear you. i know this, because of the ones i vehemently house, venture out to you often and stay gone for days on end, feeding and feasting off a particular rawness you offer. moving in and out of the quiet night, you remain the only perceptible light i have known. you are the only unruffled whisper who can break the ceiling, and give all who reside in me an assured peace that nothing will ever be the same again.

PRETENDERS

please be gentle. i am not always granite. i, too, fall into water with a mountain of fear of never coming back up. we can only hope to find ourselves before it is too late. we will taste defeat several times for every ray of light that touches us. do not worry about the losses. care only that you gave it your all. wear your wounds and scars with pride. not everyone can say they survived this life. all they can pretend to say is that they tried to live it.

When Love Becomes Lonely

everything i wish i could tell you, dies each day, again and again, as i awake to more time served than lived with you. the greatest distance i have traveled, is meeting myself, then stepping towards you, when everything i had been through told me not to. we met for a reason, even if it was in-between the dying seasons of refuge and escapism. it is something i thought i had control over. the loss and absence, the whole mess it turned out to be for me. it is a funny thing when you lose someone. sometimes, they do not miss a beat and keep going. i am not sure how it works that way, but it seems to be my entire life's story. walking skeletons in my house on leashes so they do not pull me away before i am ready to bury them indefinitely. all we can hope for is a shift for us to finally be okay with things not being okay. we are made for moving forward, because it is what we always do when salvaging breaks your will to stay. no matter how much you believed they loved you and needed you, they keep going. i thought i could replace whomever you had lost at the time, and become someone you surely needed, but you did not need me to be anything other than a distraction until things were in your favor to go back to what was safe and comfortable. it is always uneasy when your heart loves more than anything else. when you have lived your entire life believing your heart would not break you, then it ultimately does, because at some point, your ribs decide to give way to the mangled outcome. the redirection tends to become a directed relation when parallels become evenly placed and laid. if whatever love i have left comes up lost, may it always find its way back to you, through poetry, through actions,through the miles left for me to wander.

Currents We Rage Against

there is a time to die, but it will not be now, not yet. when i was younger, i met the devil before he knew who i was. i could tell he was afraid. i could tell he would never come close to taking what i had already made. the only silver spoon i had, was the one i stole and used to feed myself and those i knew. love knows your struggle, and lord knows i have been suffering through it all. broken glass has been my only mirror to show me a reflection of any kind. maybe i have been considering too much in hindsight and not enough in hardened goodbyes. being cautious is meant for those who never get to know themselves. i am and have been too far ahead of the curve to see the next bend in the road. i was born to be all out, no breaks, and only a gas pedal pressed further down. i will take my precious time when nature calls upon me to notice and take in the differences between you and every other complex living thing made of light and shine. you are an architect's wet-dream, Einstein's contested theories, and every page Fitzgerald wrote for Zelda before their boat raged on against the currents. all we tend to be are green lights in someone else's story, someone else's colorless and tasteless dreams. please, sweet emotion, have mercy on us. for we do not know how much death it takes to understand how much life should be given in return to value to a sharpened breath.

When Love Was You

i know i have not had the best relationship with love. as often as it has almost put me in the ground, the last breath i will ever take will be because of what it gave to me. i am connected and tied to it forever. growing up without such a thing, makes one become obsessive about it, writing notes for it to read when no words spoken out loud feel good enough to scream. my curse is not a curse. this world makes you believe it is, because it is easier being cold and ruthless rather than showing any ounce of adoration for what you care about. my life has been shaped and preserved by its presence and absence. my homely heart has carved out refuge any chance it could take in abandoned structures, fragmented and displaced bodies, desperately denied feelings, and anything resembling what it once was before lies rotted them all out. i wish to believe we are all here for a specific reason. i wish to believe in alimental magic, spells, and abiding connections meant to make us better. i wish to believe in giving your best effort to someone, and it not working out being a triumph of some kind. lessons become humans, and those pieces you will never be able to lose throughout your lifetime. i want to have someone say, "i love you, too." each time i think i do, profound and out-of-tune strangers overtake our bodies. we become another failed attempt at becoming something more than walking amusement parks, destined to decay. i do not know why certain humans haunt us and keep us from ever giving our maximum efforts to someone else. i have seen a million faces all staring back at me, but yours is the one i will always recognize. it has been that way since we met. eyes of fire, a bonafide holy light. body of sex itself, a walking magazine full of pages with your sun-soaked skin and familiar sin aligned in the centerfold. i kissed your hands and learned a new prayer, an unforgettable quest to locate and destroy any thought similar to the privation of faith. when you came into my life, i knew angels walked through hell to find those who could not escape it themselves. there were times when i was a child, i would wonder how often we had to suffer in order to make a life worthy of living. some days, it doesn't even feel as if thirty years gave me anything but frustration and resentment for how my life has turned out. i remind myself daily of my blessings, my victories. i remind myself you once loved me, too. I remind myself how it felt to actually have someone look you in the eyes and take in your colors and energy without looking around elsewhere to find what they could not see. you were the open road basked and frayed with moonlight to guide what remained of me home. everything seemed to be better when you were close, nearly setting aside the parts of me i had no control over when you were not around. i wanted it to mean more than it did, and you, well, you wanted to make it through the night, knowing you had someone to talk to when the sun did its rise. i became nothing more than a timeout for you, a distinct pause in-between a breath you were holding in and the scream you were born with. five years went by, and you ended it all by never telling me, goodbye. love does something to us when it is finished with us. after it has consumed and gnawed every bone we are made of, it forgets the flowers at the grave.

Ripened Age

i was not afraid. i was a young lad caught
up in a renegade made up to be man-made
disbelief. i once lived as if it were my last
day. i now live as though it is the first of
many. years pass before me, sweeping
sunsets under the rug and pitching tents
to seek rest and refuge. i burn for
consuming more than being held hostage
by the world's rule that your life is over
before you turn forty-two. simplicity reeks
in this city, and i will wander until the
soul is aired out.

Strangers & Feathers

down dirt roads where stories are half-told, but love is full. it is where kids leave their youth behind, find a pair of warm arms to keep a night from dying, held so tight. where a kiss from a girl you like turns you into a man before the moon turns you back in the world again. salvation is found where soul meets pleasure, where human finds wander. may you stumble upon every avenue of it, with trees made of golden leaves and birds with halcyon feathers. deepen your love for self and watch the entire fucking universe within you change with it.

21 Gun Salute

i sit with my grief daily, as often as i can to know it better, to memorize the names it goes by. i know i will not have the capacity most of the time to take in what else may find me that day, but we owe it to ourselves and only us to learn from it. it is a duty i will salute when it is laid to rest. my pain is mine alone, but with it, comes an unfiltered acceptance.

Ten And Twelve

i am still learning how to be patient when i want to go further from where i am now. some days, it feels as though i am dying here, awaiting the sun to fall beside me due to the orange leaving its body and the red leaving mine. i keep my mind and thoughts as positive as i can, because it does not take much for me to begin spiraling within. distractions are welcomed, but not just any kind. they all must benefit my search for a new feeling to translate, for a new road to travel and write my poetry on. i wait for the perfect moment when the blinker never gets used or thought about. when you keep the wheel at twelve, and drive into the sunset set out before you.

Chapter 7

-Stories-

Today is Friday which is the last one for this August. The month has flown by. I swore I was just on here and it was the first of the month. I do not know if I am wishing these days away or if it's what happens when we age and grow alongside the day. I recall being a kid and never realizing the true identity of a day. They all seemed to be a re-run of sorts, which has not changed as I have gotten older. I know why it is this way for me now. If you are not living the life you want, being stuck where you do not want to be, you will never get out of the mindset and see the day for what it is. I do not take them for granted. Do not get me wrong. I simply am not in a place I wish to be and have not felt at "home" since my father and I moved here back in 2017. Before this house, the last one we lived in felt more of a "home" to me. Maybe it was due to it being newer, in a better area of this part of Texas. It was honestly a beautiful place. There was a State park there, Goose Island. It was such a large area to ride your bike on or go for an ocean walk on the seaside pathway. I was happy there in a sense, but I was still heavily drinking when I was there. I arrived back at my dad's place in 2010 in such a fog full of aggression and built up anger for how everything happened and ended for me in my Marine Corps career. It stayed with me for over five years. I had never been miserable in my life, but when you are drunk all the time, you hardly notice your life falling apart. I began working out the day I got back to my dad's place. I would only drink on the weekends, which I thought was a good way to reward myself for how much I had done that week. But when I drank, I fucking demolished every bottle, can, or cup that had alcohol in it. There never has been such thing as moderation for me. Thirty beers was never enough. An entire bottle of whiskey was never enough. Nothing ever satisfied me or filled in the fucking hole inside of my soul. That is why I developed such a high tolerance for alcohol. I started at a young age and the acquired taste was something that was passed down from my mother's side of the family. It was in my blood even as a child, before I had my first sip when my parents owned an ice house in New Braunfels, Texas. I was raised around it, and living in Texas, it went with anything and everything. Fast forward over thirty years later, two DUI's, a failed suicide, mental breakdown, and a ton of other things that have happened to me because of the abuse I put my body through, I am now sober for almost 8 years now. I never thought I could quit anything to be honest. My addictive personality is a breed all on its own. I smoked cigarettes until I was thirty and began doing that when I was eleven on and off. There have been days since being back from Utah, when all I wanted to do was curl up in a fucking ball and just be left alone. I have been battling depression in low and high forms now for about a year or so. It has not been anything I could not manage, but I know it is there and has been there since I was young. I have days when I want and need to do things, but I find or make excuses as to why I do not get anything done besides writing a little bit. The weather we are experiencing now does not help either. We will be in this kind of summer until the end of September. Between the heat, humidity, and groundhog day nature I continue finding myself in, insanity is a close friend that holds my hand as I live my life here. But in a good way if that is possible to believe. My writing has never been better. I am happy, even if my writing or thoughts showcase a different side of me. When you find yourself being stuck or in the same place for years on end with no end to it in sight, you begin to believe it will always be that way, that you will never feel or find your way out. I am an optimistic human at my core, and I know nothing in this world lasts forever, not even the hardest and darkest days. There is an end to it all. There is an awakening that takes place, a pull on your energy, a subtle nudge to lead you to the next path and chapter. Patience is what ultimately separates us most from one another in this rat-race called living. Finding balance in an unbalanced world is the challenge for me. It feels as though I can never do enough or be enough for someone else, even if I at times struggle with the concept for myself. It hasn't been easy when you are raised to doubt yourself and always be the helper for everyone else. I do what I can with the gift to write to maximize my efforts in a more abstract approach. Social media has made it damn near impossible for my books to be seen by everyone who follows my work now. Thankfully, I have a support group who is there for me constantly. They do more than I could ever imagine when it comes to supporting my work and buying anything I do. Not everyone is that lucky. I know artists who sell maybe ten to fifteen copies of their books. I hate to bitch and complain about something as simple as that, but when it is your livelihood and not just some hobby you enjoy doing, it becomes necessary for you to find those or others to find you and connect to your work in a way for you to be at peace with the whole thing. It usually takes me four to six months to write these books. Which means I will need to make at least a quarter of a year's salary within a month or a few months to even compensate for the time and energy I have put into the project. I do it for the pure joy and love for writing first and foremost. Everything else that comes from it is an added bonus. I wish I was set up financially to write for free, but sadly, that is not the case as of now. Maybe one day. My dream is to travel full-time and take this on road and do pop-up shops with my typewriter and write for anyone who shows up. I do not want to be famous and I do not do this for fame of any kind. I kept my face hidden from social media for close to five years before showing it and allowing everyone to see who it was behind the screen that creates the writings. It is a spiritual experience for me. This entire process is a vulnerability not many have the balls for, which is why I do all I can to ensure my writings are as soulful and authentic as they can be. Relatability was never something I wanted my writings to be, though it is only inevitable for them to connect with others on a deeper level. Since we are all connected beyond this world, we all grow up in similar situations and households. The only person I ever wrote for was for myself and someone I loved more than anyone I had ever met. I still find myself writing for her occasionally because when you love someone as I loved her, they remain with you, embedded and twisted in everything you are and consist of. They follow you. They become something greater than the sun and moon. An immortalization of flesh and bone you will never be able to rid yourself of. The curse of love is a motherfucker, regardless of how careful you are letting someone in to get to know you, the real you, the one that is away from the screen, typewriter, computer, and in an environment of real and true world proportions. I am a nomad at heart, a true wanderer of parcels others never wish to step foot on. I am different and never hide the fact that I am. I do not care what others think about me, because I am as real as it gets when it comes to blood on paper. There is no other way for me to be, and no one will ever fucking take that away from me. My honesty is too honest. My stubbornness is too stubborn. My love is too much love, but if I am anything, I am an over-doer. I have been since my parents gave me my name. If you are not all out for life, for love, for adventure, for something greater than what is behind and in front of you, we will never mesh or see eye to eye. I do not mix my words when it comes to my aspirations. I will make it happen. I will become one of the greatest writers this world has ever seen or known. I genuinely believe that. Not because I am better than anyone else, but because I am not afraid of being judged or having my words of soul read by someone who may get offended by something I write or say out loud. We all have our goals and reasons as to why we do what we do. Mine are simple. The reasons simply mean more to me than the alternative, because I have given my entire life to this profession. I have no time to waste when it comes to creating, even though I procrastinate often, there is a rhyme and reason for it. I overload all of my senses to create the most beautiful art I can, for the reader, for myself. If I cannot write the way I live and see, I am not doing anyone justice. I am failing as a writer if I am not constantly making you feel something, making you see something in a different way. It is why I spend my time alone and away from other people's energies. I only allow a few close to me, and even then, I am standoffish. My life is not for everyone to consume first hand, but when it comes to writing about it, it is a free for all, and that is what and how I want my words to be consumed. There is nothing more important to me than to write the truth as well as I can. I have lived to much of a rough and hardened life not to be as truthful as I can when it comes to these words leaving my soul for you to read. If I can leave anything behind in this world, there is no greater treasure for me to let go of than these books I write for others to find one day. I took some much needed time away from here the last several days. Today is Thursday and the last day in August. There was a hurricane that hit Florida yesterday, Idalia. It made landfall as a weakened Category 4, though some of the news outlets reported it was a Category 3. Regardless of its intensity, it was a tremendous storm that has killed and ravaged the Florida Bend with close to and over 130mph winds. The news coverage has been spotty since it happened. I was thinking about how reporters cover stories before and up until it is over, then go back to their stations where they are from to ready themselves for another leading story. I think about how we leave people the same way in some regards. At least some of us do. We go onto the next thing, someone to fix or save, someone to create and use as art, then when we are done with the project at hand. We feel good enough and satisfied to leave them better than we found them. That thought just recently came to my mind today watching the reporting going on and around Florida. But nonetheless, it is something as simple as that which makes us all a bit cowardice at times. I understand it is not the reporters job to stay and help rebuild what has been destroyed. I just found a parallel to humanity and the disasters which find us. There is never a right or wrong time to leave should you need to or decide to. I know you did not intend on leaving me, but you never made your intentions known until I moved and got closer at providing a new life for myself and for you. Something you could be proud of. Something you could see yourself being a part of as before when I was still living with my father and you asked me about my five year plan. I made some bullshit thing up, but it was a logical thought process as to how I could be with you, while giving you the security we both needed. You chose someone else. You chose someone else's safety. To this fucking day, I wonder why I still talk to you when you message me. I wonder why I do not have the balls to leave you for good as you left me for a year before telling me what the fuck had happened. I never got a why, and truth be told, I never fucking want to know why you did and for how long you had been doing/planning it before you ultimately did it. I have a feeling it was before you and I ever met, but that is as far as I allow my mind to venture off into because it isn't worth my time and energy now. This year has absolutely flown by. Tomorrow is September. It is week one of College Football today. Several teams started last weekend to begin week zero. Utah and Florida play tonight, which I cannot wait to watch. I feel as though the Utes will win by at least fourteen points or so. Something else to watch besides Netflix and whatever else has been on. I am a huge cycling fan(professional bike racing). La Vuelta started last Saturday. It is a three week stage race with around 175 riders made up of around twenty plus teams of eight. They began in Barcelona and now are in the northern part of Spain. My favorite rider is not in the event itself, but the GC(general classification) group is insane. The winner of the Tour De France and the winner of the Giro are on the same team. They are the preemptive favorites. There is a rider whose name is Remco Evenepoel, who is the current leader after five stages. He is the former world champion, as well as the current time trial world champion from Belgium, and only twenty-three years old. It is a beautiful time of year for sports. The weather here has changed a little bit, especially in the mornings. Far less humidity now, which makes running for me a hell of a lot easier, less suffocating, and less suffering from the intensity that this summer once had been. The dry air reminds me of Utah and Arizona summers, with a dry heat that makes you feel as though you never sweat, but you do. It has been such a welcomed experience for this part of Texas summer to get here. It is still hot as fuck outside, with today hitting ninety-seven before noon, but it has helped cool off the house at least. It has made sleeping easier as well with nights hitting down into the mid seventies, instead of the low to mid eighties it had been since June.

Hopefully, by some time in late September, it will be bearable, but by then, we will be in Italy, so I am trying my hardest not to complain too much about the current situation. My dad finally got a haircut. I cut it for him since he had more hair than he could actually cut himself. It is getting more difficult for him to see things clearly. I wish I could afford Lasik surgery for him. I cannot remember the last time my dad had a buzz-cut, but it has taken me a bit longer to get used to seeing him with it. It almost reminds me of my recruit days in the Corps. I began buzzing my own hair when I was in high school. It was just easier for me to maintain it, but looking back on it now, I wish I still had hair to cut. Some days, I miss it, but not during these summers down here. My life has been flipped on its head since Covid hit as many have I am sure. I did not have a true plan when I came back here other than helping my dad get squared away and hopefully moved out of this godforsaken house. I have countless dreams and desires to get to. Things I think about constantly every waking day, as to how I could be living my life now, but I know I am here for a reason. I talk to my mother once a week. She always tells me to keep my patience, which I have an endless well of, but some days it fucking gets me down in the darkest of thoughts and feelings. There is always a reason why we move off and away from our parents at a certain age. I am thankful to be here and to still have my father. Do not get me wrong, but my growth as a man and human have been stunted for years now. I hate what it has done to me. No contact with other people other than going to the grocery store and seeing some familiar faces and doing small talk until I have what I need, then come back to the house. I also keep in mind that others around the world have it so much worse than I do, so perspective is key with anything you do or are going through in life. You always have to remind yourself that you are okay where you are, that you have food, money, a place to sleep, a roof over your head, and shelter that keeps your belongings safe. I could not imagine how difficult it is for those who do not have the means to live. I see the homeless here and there, but not as much as I used to. I am not sure if the city has done something with them or if they have just moved on to a different city. South Texas has numerous amount of them, and the ones I have seen, are a large majority of Vets. It kills me when I see them with their cardboard signs, asking for help of any kind. The other side of my brain always wonders if they are telling the truth or not, but I give what I can, when I can, and even donate money to the causes of all Vets. We as a society have lost track of what decency is and what it used to be. The government contracted us out to go to war for them, then when they are done with us, they discard us in the toy drive pile to forget about for good. I know several veterans who have taken their own life inside of VA and outside of them because of the lack of help they have received. It has been over two years now since I lost one of my friends to his suicide. A self-inflicted gunshot to the head. He has been the last one to end his life. Each day, I am always waiting on the next phone call to find its way to me, telling me we lost someone else. Thankfully, nothing like has happened yet since Paul. I remember when we were getting ready to leave for Afghanistan, my platoon leader got us all together and told us how different it would be for us when we got home. He said, you are a veteran now. You have will have that for the rest of your life attached to your name. When you get home, you will feel different. You will walk differently. You will act and talk differently. You will come to find out there are not many of you walking around this world. The percentage of Vets who are Marine Corps Infantry, is less than one percent of the US population. I never allowed that to get inside of my head and make it bigger than it was. I do not go about my day, boasting about it or talking about it. I have not spoken about my time in the military with anyone since I went to Paul's funeral when I got to meet up with my brothers who I had not seen in over ten years. My best friend, Ryan/Steezy, is someone I once talked to at least once a day when we finally reconnected a few years ago, but I haven't had contact with him in months. I hate what the military does to you in a lot of ways, but mostly when you get out, you lose contact with those you fought with, bled with, suffered with, and almost died with for years. It is a true brotherhood, and if I miss anything besides being in war, it is that. My life has always been a bit chaotic, so to have had that in my life it was the most constant thing I had ever experienced since my high school years. I could go on and on about the military life and what it had taught me and showed me, but I will keep it there for now. This year has been a complicated one for me, but better than the previous three. Though I am still where I am before I moved to Utah, it could always be worse as I previously stated. I do my best to keep myself in check when I feel myself heading down some depression filled thought and feeling fucking sorry for myself. I am not that kind of human. I know how lucky I am and how fortunate I am to be here with my father who helps me more than he will ever know. There are days when I wish I was alone and on my own. I do not do well at all being around someone all the time like this. I pick up on his energy and it transfers to me. I can feel when he is worried, sad, anxious, all of it. I have had that "gift" since I was a kid. It played a large part in me turning to drugs and alcohol in the first place. To feel numb is better than to feel anything at all. At least that is what I thought for over a decade. I still remember sitting outside on the deck of my best friend's house in college station after doing a few lines of meth and listening to Mercy Me(christian rock group) and staying awake for days on end. The longest I went without sleep was almost a week. I barely ate anything and was doing cocaine and meth daily it seemed. I went to college weighing over 200lbs. At one point, I was at 145lbs. Luckily, it never killed me nor did it carry over into any other part of my life, except a few times when I was twenty-three. I was in such a dark place, it felt like a place to escape to. I could write all day about it, because my memory is both a curse and gift. Some areas of my life remain blacked out and forgotten. It is that way for a reason. I choose not to remember or recall certain years of my life because of the trauma that lives there. I do not ride that elevator. I do my best to stay on the top floors and create new memories to build on so I never have to find myself in the depths of my past. Today, has been a good one for me. I ran over five miles and it has been the first time I could make two laps around the track here without stopping. I can run forever on a treadmill, but running outside has not been something I have been able to do since I was in my late twenties. My knees, back, and hips are shit now, so I need the treadmill to help reduce the energy and impact on my body. My side still hurts, near the middle part of my left side. I do not know what is wrong with it, but it has been there since 2020. I need to go the doctor, but I continue to scare myself out of it, thinking it is worse than it is, knowing the money I have saved since getting back here could all be spent because of it. With the trip coming up next month, I know I will need to get it checked out eventually. I know it will work itself out and how it needs to. Today, I have done more writing than as of late. It feels good to get it all out of you or at least most of it so you can rest comfortably knowing you have unleashed built up thoughts and ideas. I am going to go eat, then watch the bike race, and enjoy the college football later this evening.

Chapter 8

-Poetry & Prose-

BURNOUT

you will always be the California sunset and the goodbye in its sunrise. your summer shine is fading and your autumn is beginning to show. sometimes, it feels as though i am the only one who can see the blue in my eyes. i know one day, i will find the perfect words i have been looking for since birth. it seems to be the only thing that keeps me going now. i could write until my hands turned white, when all the blood turned into light, but i would still not have enough time to explain all the things creeping and hiding in my mind. i once wrote for the love i felt for someone else other than the love i had for myself. it is a mistake i will not make again. i tried forcing my words to come out of someone else's mouth and all i have to show for it are tongue lashings and whip marks along my jawline and chest. we will never be together, because you are not ready, and i do not blame you for saving what is left of your life for your own two hands to create what is next for you. i am going to hide myself from everyone for a while. i am tired and worn out by barely getting by. your memory burned me out.

When Love Becomes The Lie

i was not born like the rest of those with a pure soul, with a properly given opportunity to ultimately change an outcome without proving it. my testament became scars written out on religious beliefs that we become who we are, regardless of thinking it out loud. i pound my mighty chest, with a million fists wrapped in prose, full of incarcerated hallucinogens, often given away to seekers of a stronger drug kept by those who use it for themselves. down Abbey Road and across a fervent bridge in the middle of nowhere, is a misconception brought on by reliving a past meant for travelers who missed out on the last train home. i have fumbled my fair share of promises and unintentional love spoken clearly to be heard by anyone with ears and eyes. i am no better than the beggar on a corner looking for their next fix, the next hit of anything to make them forget about a lover. i have no needle marks, just calloused hands covered in ink and a tongue dipped in a farce about who we are when everything decides to leave us at the same time. i want to uncover truth down to its rarest form, down to its bone of structural integrity. i want to see if it will bend with the wind or get tossed around in a mouth of a newspaper town lost to another man-made tragedy. there is nothing special about me. my tattoos are therapy, even if some believe them to be a boy hiding behind insecurities handed down by his mother and father. my path is directionless, an unkempt plan discarded daily by an ever-changing array of motionless bodies pretending to know more about death than i. being centered means knowing your worth, when feeling worthless became a lifestyle to keep away those who meant you harm if you ventured too far from the middle, where they perpetually held their gatherings. when someone comes to you with their own depiction and definition of what being shattered means, a true bond is formed underneath Saturn's rings. not everyone wants love. they simply want an embrace to negate a place in their lives where agony screams out, showcasing they are still alive. i broke my truce with the angel in you to get to where i am now. i trusted you when trust gave me away like a wish saved by grace. i am here to feel alive by any means necessary, by doing what is necessary to feel loved again. if it means to be alone, isolated in my own belongings, i shall do just that. the only middle ground i am aware of, is where devils and demons showcase their collections of misplaced dreams to barter for another chance to get their wings. being in this world, you often forget how easily wars are won and lost. you often forget how tragic goodbye is when it is the last thing you hear from someone who told you they would only leave you as their last breath left them. maybe there is hope in the broken, in the brittle parts of autumn when the trees break down right in front of us to keep us aware of how precious all life is. love is a miserable thing at times. it keeps you held hostage with a gun pointed at your head, playing with empty chambers to see how well you suffer for destiny.

Too Far Gone To Know Better

there used to be a feeling here. one your hand would make upon touch, upon your closeness becoming an art-form i would stay awake to be a part of. my nights are a continuous prayer said by angels keeping me company in place of an absence i hope no one ever feels. i am made of gentle sorrows and high flying sparrows all conveying a certain truth about what exists outside of our control. my forgiveness is in its infant stages, an imperfect quality to the duality of a life mismanaged by this human i fail at being. i know we are what we say out loud and in the quiet corners of every pause we find ourselves in. i am trying to manage multiple lives within the one i am living. i am trying to make sure my sacrifices for those i love become an outlet for my words to openly grieve when they, too, feel alone by me not giving them what is needed. sometimes, my breath is the heaviest thing about me. other times, my body leans too far left because of the weight i have in my heart for those who left me. nothing happens by chance, only by choice. life, love, and death, are a magnificent trio when it comes to finding out who you are when they find you and thrust their wholeness onto your path. you cannot escape all three. we do our best with what we have and what we have lost. everything you do makes you become a variant to who you used to be back when being young was about staying that way before adulthood brought you in. i remember watching my parents happily being together, instead of the downfall they eventually became. there was something about a steady stride i could never be in sync with. i knew a steadiness would never accept me for my chaos, for my ineptitude when it came to doing the right thing when it was asked of me. maybe love lasts for those who never risk anything. maybe it is some parlor trick meant for those gullible enough to believe in something keeping us all together before the ending presents itself. i saw a young girl today in a wheelchair. maybe five or six years old. other kids were running around never knowing a thing about what life for her is like. a few adults were around her, making sure she experienced life outside of her own empathy which is the only form of love i know. it is the only form of love i will openly accept from someone else who knows nothing else about me. we are creatures of habit, and my habitual stance has never moved or changed since i was a kid, because at one point in my life, i was that kid who no one played with, talked to, or understood. i made my own world. some days, i still find myself in it, with no one else around me. it is not ideal for many to participate in, because we are programmed to be around others, to include ourselves in everything everyone else is doing. i have never found satisfaction in living that way. i may never say a word to you, even if i am standing right next to you, but i will do my best to make sure you never feel alone in any sense of the word. too many of us are that way these days. it is a sickness that goes untreated until we are too far gone.

Be Here For You

trying to remind yourself to breathe is not an easy achievement. there is a specific pattern to life that is overwhelming for the artist in me. i wake up a lot of the time feeling like a failure, but i have to remind myself how far i have come with this broken heart of mine riding shotgun alongside me. my alive day was forty-eight hours ago. i almost forgot about it until someone i love brought it up. i know why i have forgotten more than some will ever remember. i know why i am this way. i understand my place inside of the lives no longer taking up space in mine. we all get to the point of no return, when nothing you do satisfies you because you are not living your true potential. you are wasting valuable time deciding on a safe bet rather than risking one more chance to be who everyone said you could not become. do not grow old forfeiting away memories for the sake of maintaining whatever life you think you have made for yourself. i am not better than anyone walking this fucking planet, but i do have an endless supply of motivation, a work ethic that will eventually lead me to the places i am made for. i do not share much of my life on here anymore. it is a tireless frame of popularity i stopped giving a shit about a long time ago. i know what i do is enough. it took me a while to figure out that is all you need. if all i have to write about is suffering, it is because i am good at it. it is where my human is found. it is where my ache is a shared concept felt by those who have died a few thousand times to value living. i am not indestructible. i have been put together by hundreds of hands that wanted to see me be better than the excuses i gave for not trusting my scars to lead the way. i look around and see eyes that cry only when they are alone. i will embrace every emotion i have adopted in order to be as authentic as possible. vulnerability is a right of passage. mine tends to be a wildfire caught inside of a vortex of implausible conflicts no one else can see. i am at war with normalcy, with anything said without proven or shown to be true. some days. i am dangling from the sun. other days, i am in love with the moon being out while it is hanging itself thinking there is a more logical way to find love without dying before you do. there is always a better way to live before you believe all you have left to give someone is a sacrifice you cannot hand over. you are you for a reason. i can only hope one day you see that and not worry about what you do not have. we all are designed to be this version of us today. we owe ourselves the best opportunity to be at our best, because there are many who surrendered their own lives for you to be where you are today. be grateful. be whole and full on the aspect of today being enough and not fearing tomorrow because of it. you will have plenty of time down the road to look back on your life and realize you missed out on an infinite amount of memories because you were hyper-focused on the outcome of something that never will fucking matter at the end of the day. love is knowing yourself first.

Conversation With Light

we are stones cast out to sea, a wish never spoken of or heard from again. not many make it back to shore to walk on dry land or breathe in a tender sigh given by a moon's goodbye. i will sit here and drink my fire roasted bean of a hill country's salute and battle cry. views like this are not god-given or hell-made. these are from a supernova colliding with a warrior's fight. we may never get these eyes again, these hands to know right from wrong. i walk the finest of lines ever cut out, even more than the one June made Johnny stroll. all it takes is one good woman to keep you breathing. all it takes is one good woman to change what was once there before you gave into believing your heart was always made to be broken. i will love you until the Lord leaves his last supper and Mary calls him home once again. we must find ourselves in the day and somewhere in a place away from we it all began. if we do not, we will continue repeating the behaviors and outcomes that made us feel worthless to begin with. lean on your own backbone more and less on those who have used yours to straighten out theirs. your eyes deserve something beautiful to open for. i hope you never forget how the shine feels in the morning hours when it is just you and the light.

BATMAN

i remember my mother would do her best to show me how to be loved. times were lost because of an absent family, which led me down a road of self-destruction for never feeling as though i was enough. i did not drink to forget. i drank to remember what feeling nothing at all felt like. i was so pissed off all the time at the world, it bled into me believing in my own self-hatred for everything i was becoming. the devil had its own room in our home. i never disturbed it. i could hear it through the walls, screaming with conviction after the alcohol reached its tipping point, drink after bloody fucking drink. silence became a thoughtful reverie, a sobering song only i could sing after the night had died. love became synonymous with my brokenness, yet i will never give up the fight to show more of my heart to those fighting similar ghosts and demons.

A General And His Army

i will never be on stage or have anything more in my pockets than these hands that get nervous except when they find you. my voice is not my strength, but my words will forever have your name stitched and sewed perfectly within every fucking letter i type. if i could sing, every song would be the same. every word would begin with your name. when you grow up battling for your life, doing nothing hurts similarly, in ways only those who survive can describe. i have been going on thirty years of it, a general to my own troops, a cascading and reduced army due to the fatigue and battles lost. my prisoners all live within the cells i have created within me. at night, you can hear them all chanting, rebelling, beginning to approach the gates with more fervor and fire for their release. i am the battlegrounds for the defining victory of my own war raging inside of me.

My Mirror

i am after more than the stars show me to me in my darkness. i am only lost when i am away from you, away from the soul we share. if there were to be without you, take my name and face away from me. i do not belong to this place if it is not by your side. i do not belong to this place if it is not me telling you, i love you, in one form of expression or another. my body only feels right when it is next to you, near you, close enough to feel you breathe when i do.

ASTRONAUT

i never knew how to be anything more than
who i was before you. a lifetime of wondering
has left me scattered amongst a less assorted
assembly of perfection. we could spend half the
day on the phone, then the very next day, do
the exact same thing. without living near one
another, we always had something new to say,
express, and share with the other. our days
were never boring, without need of the other.
i do not know how we lasted for as long as
we did, but i am finally at a place in my life
where i can say i am thankful it all happened,
because it saved me from a life of nonexistence
and floating around in my own world without
a reason to ever come back down to put my feet
back on solid ground to walk on my own for
once. the grass feels cool again and the dawn
left its tears it cried for me upon my arrival.

When You Were Here

love may never feel like this again, as if the
sun itself fell from the sky and landed in
your heart. there is a fire the gods once
spoke about. i am trying to remember how
not to run away, but remain firmly
pressed against an unending sensation
of unexpected and righteous alignment.

ATHENA

dreams of another life keep her up at night. maybe somewhere in nature or a place by the ocean where no one knows a single thing about her. hard times have strengthened a heart bruised and broken by many. she is every city she has ever been to. each brick represents a foundation found within the bones she carries. the light always finds her and the losses she has had to keep inside. we all go through life differently, but she is of the rarest kind. bright eyes and a panoramic smile all the time, an infinite armor for getting by when those around her get too close to a story not ready for the ending they end up choosing for her. there is gold in the broken, a silver lining of stubbornness in hoping for a gleaming day when breathing stops the hurting she was forced to live out. she is morning's light for all of us left behind the sun to burn alone.

Texas, Arizona, Utah, California

please take these hands of mine and make them whole again, make them strong again. show them how to hold onto what they never have held before. show them how to keep yours inside this clench, evermore. there needs to be more warmth inside of them, more softness around them, and more of you all over me. i am covered in the excess of what life has done to me, unmercifully. i have been buried all over the country, digging myself back up every time your voice began to crack and weaken. i come to you as a friend now. i had to leave the lover i was for you in the last grave your goodbye left me in. never again will i reach that point of death for someone else who gives up looking for me when i need a few minutes to rest my mind and eyes of searching for myself.

The Dream After The Dream

you are the impression on my heart, as well as the one it holds inside of it with a care and adoration i am unfamiliar with. i have gone so long without considering meeting someone again, i never saw you coming. i am beaming about it. it has been a total reshaping of the exterior and interior of who i thought i was before you. some days, i pretend to be busy in my mind just so that i am not messaging you more than you would like. it is a beautiful issue for me to have, since you now live in these writings of mine. the other day, you were by the lake with your feet in the water, watching airplanes take off and land about a mile away. you had just returned from running errands and you wore that smile so well. i could see you happy, and i have wondered what yours looked like. now, i know it to be the sun and moon in love, meeting for the first time all over again. in my mind, i ran to you and picked you up just as the wind carries new love each day it is given reason to. i never saw my middle having someone who looked like you. someone who was all brightly made up with moonly hues. you may never allow me to be closer than a dream to you, but you are worth everything to me. you are worth the suffering i once endured, wondering if i would find someone who found it to be as worthy as it had made me become.

It's Okay Not To Know Where This Road Goes

this life is not easy, and it is not for those who believe it be that way. i do not find common ground with those who have never struggled. those who have never had to wonder where their next meal was going to come from. those who have walked by the homeless and thought, that could never be me. i hope for so many things these days, an easier breath to breathe, a quiet but fearless smile, a taste of sunlight that does not burn parts of me i have already given to this fight. i have been caged and forgotten. i have driven over two thousand miles just to feel love and see if it was different than what someone once showed me before. the smallest act of affection goes a long way with me, because more than half of my life, i had gone without anything resembling love itself. it was difficult for me to be held, to be spoken to softly at all. there is still a kid in me i am trying to save daily, for him to know we made it, finally. i am at my worst when i am giving too much, because i know where that leads. i know where it ends. my confusion is the next example as to who i am, and what life does to you if you never leave those who leave you first. replacing yourself never gets easier.

The Haunting That Never Comes

where do i know you from? a dream, a past-life, a lifetime ago, a stranger i passed on some beat down street and has yet to leave me? i lift my hands to the sky above and the sun moves for me. i had asked you during this preview of an encounter if you had any memory of me that you would like to add to, and all i heard was you telling me, you missed me. some days, i am nothing more than bird's eyes catching colors before the night dies. other times, i am someone who swears they fucking love you, each time i pass you underneath the moon's eyes. i am at best, miserable and wretched, a broke clock showing the same time, the same moment of when it all happened to you and i. in my dream, i keep turning right as you go left. o wake up missing a ghost i do not know what to do with when it is not haunting me.

Until It All Ends

i have tried writing you into my life for a while now, centered and imagined so vividly, i swore you were the morning light itself and the fawn-like embers from the fire we had to create. my life has been nothing but chaotic, a new intensity for every year i had survived. i am made up of hellish clusters and forgotten relics of a past where everything died before getting a fair chance to properly live. you may not want anything to do with me and these scars i do not hide anymore. you may see my grief to be more than your own or ever wish to be around. i would like to sit with you on your deck and watch a day be born and slowly fade, giving away all of our secrets to one another during its boundful retreat. may our dreams one day blanket our bones and all that remains of two humans who have been to all seven rings only to become one within each other's hand. i cannot promise that much anymore these days that i have not already lost, but i can hold you until your mind becomes silenced and free. i can hold you until the world stops spinning and the stars fall beneath our feet.

Chapter 9

-Stories-

I know the next part of my life is going to take everything I have already given before today. Each finger pressed onto these keys creates space for more memories and leaves behind a smoldering trail of death for where I have been. I do not know how to be anything other than a wandering blaze, a profuse preponderance of perplexing parodies. I need more than a life where you come home to the same place you can barely sleep in. I need more than having someone you love never ask or dig deep enough to extract your soul. My life has never gone the way I had hoped it would go. Occasionally, some twist of fate and cosmic aligning has taken place. Those are days that give my words blood and thick skin. Those are days a sacrifice is given by kindly exchanging emotions for numbness. I have to be some times to know what it feels like when your best days are because of a particular loss you never thought you would be capable of living without. I have always given my heart away without a proposal, a swift interchangeable direction of a needle-less compass. I have found in this lifetime how everyone you meet will be able to tell you who they are and why they do what they do. It feels as though I have skipped my way from circus to circus, collecting souvenirs from the acts I felt I had something in common with. My life is not a tragedy nor is it a comedy. It remains a rough sketch of a man meeting himself day in and day out, hoping the same two versions never see each other. I do not want complacency anywhere near who I am. If you are not working on yourself or what you love, we already have nothing in common or anywhere to begin. My lessons found me with each friend I have lost over the years. They have given me internal perspective of what it takes if you want to make it further down the void we all call life. We must find a passion before a nothingness takes from us what we have already given too often to an empty corridor, full of doors that showcase "do not disturb" signs nailed to the front of them. I may not be enlightened enough to know myself from what a mirror tells me I am. I can tell the difference between those who look to find discrepancies and those who see higher meaning. I have looked wolves in the eyes and backed down to none. I am the fear you feel. Maybe love is hidden away behind the winter grass and fallen trees, out beyond the sun where blue remains a constant state of purity without clouds to cover up what has been done to its effort. Trails encompass us all, made from footprints of wanderers hoping to find safety from the wind. Chapped lips and hands become a look of life when you have been without shelter for this long. I know there is a place for common ground where humans make mistakes, but feel as though it is who they should become and remain. I am too in love with what is around me to ever stay in my center for long. My hands stretch out beyond the perimeter others have set to keep refuge as company and friend. I understand why many of us flinch at the word after all of the bruises and scars we have accumulated along this journey. My hesitation does not exist within your arms, your kiss, your enchantment. My wounds are not yours to fix or heal. My life is not yours to live. Somewhere together is where we will find what we need. Past the snow covering bones of who we used to be, still frozen with regret and a fondness for comfort we have yet to find. Give me peace, and I will give you what is left of the clay others tried to store away until they were ready to mold me into what they felt as though I should give them in the first place. I have no use for ghosts and other shades of light when I know who you are is what I have been missing my entire life. This idea we speak about with one another when both of our bodies are submitted underneath covers, is the exact spot I hope to always wake up in. A warmness no other human could give me, you provide with an ease I think you do not even comprehend, because you were never made aware of your love for the one you were with. I think of life differently than most. I was never born to be a copy and paste kind of human. I enjoy what we are and who we are when easy silence uncovers the truest intent. Between us, there is no such thing as an uncomfortable approach to loving. Every single thing we do is an act of freewill, an uncommon bond for the souls we share. My feelings rise with the sun. Even if it means being up before you, you sleeping is an image of safety for me.

Today is Friday the 8th, a day before my 38th birthday. I am unsure if I feel older, but I know my body is getting there. I woke up two days ago with a stiff neck and it has been aggravating me ever since. Today is a little better and a bit less pain, but nonetheless, age is motherfucker. I know tomorrow I will be receiving phone calls and messages for most of the day from my immediate family and those who know it is my birthday. I am not one who celebrates my birthday as others might. I went to the store today and bought four red velvet cupcakes and added a few candles to them. I will eat two of them and give the remaining ones to my dad to have. It has been a tradition I started a few years ago with the cupcakes. Growing up, I think the last true meaningful birthday celebration I remember was around seven or eight. I was in Los Banos, California. I was living in a motel room with my mom, dad, and brothers. We had flown out there to see my dad because he had been working there for over a year and he wanted us to come and see him. It was my first plane trip that I remembered. It was a gnarly experience for a kid my age.

There was this older woman sitting next us and she asked me if I wanted any gum to chew so my ears would not pop. I had no idea what the hell she was talking about. I asked my mom and she said it was okay. All four of us ended up chewing gum for the entirety of the trip which was around three plus hours. We landed in Sacramento and my dad picked us up and drove us back to the motel. I recall seeing palm trees lining the road, the sun being as bright as I had ever witnessed before. My birthday happened to be the month after we got there. I made a birthday gift list, which included a toy gun and Under Siege. It is a movie that had Steven Segal in it who was one of my favorite actors at the time because of his karate and action scenes in all of the movies he played in. There was a movie rental place a few blocks down from where we were staying. My dad rented a VCR and the movie so I could watch it. He had also bought me a plastic M-16 that I used every day after that. I am laughing out loud as I am typing this because of how vivid the memory still is for me. My mother began teaching us while we were there so we could be ready for the next school year when we got back to Texas. There were days of flash cards, homework, and reading anything she thought would help us. it was such an innocent time back then because of how the world was. My two brothers and I would walk to 7/11 every morning with her. She would get herself some coffee and we were allowed to pick out one comic book for the week to read as a reward for the schooling. I always got The Punisher comics. My older brother went for Superman or Spiderman. My younger brother went for X-Men. On Fridays, we were allowed to get a slurpie, which was a big deal to us, because they were the best thing about Fridays. While we were, we began watching X-Files when it first came on TV. It was one of the best shows ever created and still is to this day. My parents would be in their bed and we would walk over through the door that separated our rooms to watch it as a family. Some of the best moments of my life have happened in motel rooms, both young and old. Out of every birthday I have had, that is one of the ones that sticks out most to me. We ended up staying there for two months before leaving. We would not see our father again for another year or so. One other particular birthday that sticks out to me, is my 9th birthday. I got home from school and my mom had baked a cake for me. She had it all set up and ready on the kitchen table. It was one of the few times we had actually used that table since we ate all of our food at the counter bar we had. I got to go to C&D Video, which was the movie rental place in our small town. I grew up in a place with less the 3,500 hundred people. There was no Blockbuster or large rental stores for us, but they always had the movies we wanted to see and would hand out posters from the movie itself. I chose, The Ref, for my birthday. It was a christmas movie, but was located in the comedy section. It has Denis Leary in it, and he is a thief that tries to steal a diamond from a house and ends up tripping the alarm system. He is left there by his partner and is on his own until he goes to a small convenience store and kidnaps a couple. The entire movie is insane. It is and remains one of the funniest movies I have ever watched to this day. It is by far a top five for me and easily a top Christmas movie. It is rated R, so if you get offended by that sort of thing, do not watch it. My parents were lenient with us growing up as to what we could watch. It seemed to be that way for a lot of kids back in the day. I watched Jaws when I was five or six. I watched Rambo and anything else Rated-R you could think of before I was ten. My vocabulary was full of profanity before I was ten. I learned sarcasm at a young age and other things as well. I stopped celebrating my birthday after that year I believe. My parents would end up getting a divorce a few years after that. We were basically a make-shift family for around five years, until I was ten or eleven, which is when the split happened. I say that to say this, I do not need to celebrate my day of birth as I once did or as others do. I am just as happy with red velvet cupcakes and college football games all day. The greatest thing about my birthday now, is the joy I get from being alive and being able to purchase something if I feel as though I need to. I am not a fan of all the calls and messages. I have never been one for the spotlight or acknowledgment of any kind. I am better suited for the low-key type of lifestyle with no one really knowing what I am doing or what they think they should celebrate about me. I celebrated my birthday with my father on Saturday by doing nothing but watching College Football all day, which is my favorite sport in the world. Texas played Alabama in Tuscaloosa. Texas was a seven point underdog and won 34-24. It was not even that close, but nonetheless, one of the greatest sporting days of my life happened that night. I lost my voice. My dad was riled up, which is always a funny dynamic because he hardly ever gets fired up for sports these days. I had eaten my red velvet cupcake before the game began. I added eight candles to it in a representation of turning thirty-eight. I made my wish and then blew out the candles. I had wished for a Texas victory. I know, lame, I am sure you are thinking, but as a diehard Texas fan, it had been mediocre for over a decade. This was their biggest win since the National Championship with Vince Young as their quarterback. I stayed up until 1:30am on such a high. I could not sleep. Sunday brought more football, and the

NFL christened their season after the Thursday night game between the Lions and Chiefs, which the Lions won. The Dallas Cowboys played last night and beat the New York Giants, 40-0. Their biggest blowout in the history of the rivalry. It was the best sporting weekend for me in probably fifteen years. Going back to me not being a huge advocate for my own birthday, I do appreciate those who reach out to me to let me know they care. It is a special day. I just do not give it much thought because for me, every day is a type of celebration in a way for still being alive after my suicide attempt, after coming home from almost eight months at war, after finally finding sobriety. Once you go to war, it changes you and your perspective on things, but I have always thought differently than most just because of my upbringing and who I was then, and who it turned me into. I celebrate often other people's birthdays more than my own because it matters to me more than my own. I love everyone in my life to the extreme, and when their day rolls around, it brings me great joy to be financially able to give them something they typically do not receive in their everyday life. Today is September 11th. The morning brought a grief back to me just as every anniversary does on this day. I recall everything from that day. Where I was. What I was wearing. What I was doing. The weather. The sounds. The people I was around. The classroom I was in. All of it comes rushing back to me, and I am back in the classroom, sitting in my desk, watching the TV. This was before social media, so the TV was our only way of knowing what was going on in the world. I always have found it to be odd to celebrate my birthday since that day because two days later, terrorists murdered 2,977 Americans. To this day, there are those still dying because of illnesses, cancer, and mental health. The grief from that day hangs onto those like the blackest cloud in the sky, and will never leave. It changed everyone's life moving forward. I do my best to remember that day, because of the importance it played in not only my life, but everyone else's that day. I had always wanted to join the Marines when I was a kid. I knew then it was my destiny. The attack only added to it. If I could have joined then,

I would have. It would not be until another five years for me to have the chance to enlist into the Marines. The weather has begun to change for the cooler. You can feel it in the air. Though it is still in the nineties here, the humidity has dropped. I believe it was almost at fifty percent this morning when I went for my run. It is still insanely hot here for this time of the month. We are finally on the other-side of it. I cannot be any happier about it. Fall is my favorite season. Texas does not have four seasons as some of the states do. There is a noticeable change in the weather normally near the midpoint of this month or the third week into it. This book as with, SONDER, has turned into more of journal than an actual book I am writing, which I find to be even more therapeutic in a lot of ways. When I use my typewriter, the writings are different than those I hand-write or when I use captions on Instagram. In a lot of ways, I have three or four writing styles compared to the singular one someone would use to write or use in their journal. Each one represents a different side of me, a different level of openness and comfort in the words I use and feel as though I can share. My hopes are with the trip to Italy coming up, I will be able to go there and leave my phone alone and simply live in the moment, type, journal, and see life for what it is. It has been since November of 2019 when I was alone and in my solitude. I fucking miss it daily. I love my father, yes, but there is a reason why we leave our parents eventually. It is for us to grow as humans and create the vision for ourselves as to what we want and who we want to become. When I lived in Utah, I found myself. I was able to get my tattoos, write freely, and be myself unfiltered. Being here, I feel as though it has stunted my growth in so many ways, but it has also allowed me to save enough money for when it is time to be on my own again I will be able to do so comfortably. This life I am currently living is not the ideal situation for creatives. There are hurdles and obstacles to get over and through on a daily basis. The constriction of creation is such a detrimental aspect of being around your parents when you are older like this, living day in and day out with them. At least for me that is how I feel. One of these days it will change. I am not here to be forty years old, taking care of my father. As much as I love him, I know he knows that is not what he wants from me either. Tonight, the Buffalo Bills play the New York Jets on Monday Night Football. It should be an amazing game. The experience and vibe from it will be a beautiful reminder and remembrance of the day twenty-two years ago. I am looking forward to seeing the tribute and homage they pay for those and to those who lost their lives and whomever they bring to the game to honor. These days are flying by. I talked to my uncle the other day on my birthday. We were joking around about how quickly the years go by after thirty. We reminisced about the early years of my life and how much time I spent at my grandmother's house(Mimi.) It seems like the other day, my brothers and I were sleeping on the floor in the living room of their home with my grandfather at the kitchen table reading the paper and my grandmother getting breakfast ready in the kitchen. They had french doors with openings you could look through to see what was going on while being secretive about it. the smell of her biscuits, gravy, bacon, jams, jellies, and sausage, will always be something I can close my eyes and smell to this day. It is humorous what we recollect and can still recall as vivid as the day it happened. They are my true and core memories. The good, bad, and indifferent. There is an illimitable beauty in there somewhere as well. The best days of my life always had some type of tragically placed event happening that led to more beauty finding its way to me. The day after September 11th is always a different feeling for me when it comes to grieving and mourning those who were lost then, and those who have been lost in the war and the aftermath of everything that happened with the illnesses and cancer to those searching all for all the months after. It is another blue sky day here, same as it was the day after the towers fell. When it comes to remembering events in my life, there seems to be a trigger mechanism like in most humans. All it takes is a single smell, color, glance, feeling, placement, and everything comes pouring back in, as if I were a coloring book being covered in paint over every black line and image. It is the most intense, and most of the time, most satisfying release of thought one can have. I typically get one of those a day. I can be sitting, looking into the blankness of life itself, then be captivated by something or someone. The art in me never changes. It will remain there for as long as I am alive and breathing. The well it all sits in, never runs dry no matter how many times I go to it for inspiration. I was born to create what I see and feel. That declaration is not me being egotistical or self-absorbed. It is me knowing who I am and my purpose. I hope one day we all can arrive to that point of awareness and know why we are here. I hope one day we all can come to the conclusion that anything created by us is a singular purpose many will never achieve. It can come in many different forms and an array of subject matters, but I did not need to go to college for someone to tell me this is what I should or should not be doing. I have never allowed someone else's influence to dictate what it is I should be doing. Of course, I have read certain poetry books that influenced me, but those were by dead poets. They are the only kind of poets and poetry I read and have ever read. Anyone can write anything and call it a best seller these days, because they put it into a category on Amazon no one uses or describes correctly. Some only sell ten copies and promote themselves as such. It is a disgrace to the profession. I cannot stand those who do that. If you have to or feel the need to lie about the quality of your book and work, you are not any better than those who profit from stealing someone else's work. If I have read something years ago that I see in your work now, and you claim it to be yours, and you believe it is your conscious work, you are one of the worst and most deplorable humans in existence. The single sentences and micro-poetry that gets taken and shared by thousands is such a travesty. I will never understand why you share or even write it if it is nothing more than a thought we all have had before. If you are not attempting something new and original, do not take time to be a thief of the art. I see it way too often these days. It is why I never read what someone else living says poetry wise, because more times than not, it is all regurgitated or they change a word here and there, claiming they did it all on their own. I did not meant to get on a tangent about this, but this is what I have given my life to. It is my livelihood and my passion. It matters to me that we as humans and individuals, become who we need to be, doing what we need to do, and nothing getting in the way of coming up with our own ideas and paths. We sacrifice so much to get to this point of living and dying daily just for someone to read something we wrote or look at something we have painted. I am not here to waste someone's precious time on something I do not wholly believe in. I am not here to cheat the human reading it and I am depriving myself from growth as an artist. When I was getting closer to graduating high school, my entire family would ask me what I wanted to be and what college I was going to. I never had a real answer for them. This one time when I was fifteen or sixteen, my older brother, younger brother, my dad and I, all took a road-trip to Arizona so we could all fly out together to celebrate Christmas in St. Croix. My father was dating this woman who lived there and we were all going to meet her before we flew out a few days later. my older brother was in his senior year in high school, and the whole trip, my dad was battering him with questions about college. I got so sick of hearing them talk and argue back and forth. I knew then, I would have the same argument/conversation with him a few years later when I was my brother's age. It took us about a day and a half to finally get tot Arizona, but by the time we did, it was all done with. I could not have been happier knowing that part of the trip was over. I knew early on I was not going to college, and if I did, I would not be there for long. I had always wanted to be in the Marines. I used to wear my dad's old USMC shirts, as well as his dog tags. I was born to be a Marine. Even as a child, I was outworking and doing more than those older than me. It was my destiny. A few years later, it was my turn to be harassed and ridiculed about where I was going and what I would be doing. I know it is something every teenager gets asked and tormented over. I was never concerned with it, because my plan was to enlist when I was eighteen. I tried the college life for a few years and after the agreement my father and I had, I volunteered in December of 2006. Looking back on it now, I would have been retired already from the military if I had chose to remain and act as I should have while I was in and not get discharged. I would be thirty-eight with an entire career behind me, multiple combat tours. I would be getting my benefits monthly. I chose the hard way, as I had my entire life. It has never been easy for me. From birth, until now, the formidable line has always been crossed by me, regardless of where it was drawn or located. I am Icarus if anyone ever were to be him. I did not fly too close to the sun. I flew as quickly as I could directly into it, time and time again. I ate the entire fucking ball of fire and light just to know what it felt like to do something someone told me I never could. I was never bothered by the outcome, because I knew my path would reveal itself to me eventually. After the failed suicide attempt I had in 2009, I knew my life would never be the same again. I was right. Everything changed because I could not handle the reality of which I was living in. I do not know if I will ever get accustomed to this life. It is why I chose to write again and why writing found me once more in 2014. I started sharing more of my work in 2013, but it did not become something I thought could take me any place higher than I already was. But for once in my life, I trusted it all without me getting in the fucking way of it. I gave my all to it to end up here, doing what I love to do now as a job. Most likely, it will not make me a rich man, but it has made me a more grateful man, a more aware human, and a man finally connected to his own soul. It is my hope for everyone to locate that one thing or multiple things they are good at, then ultimately sharpen it day after day. We owe it to ourselves to be happy. We are the choices behind it. We are our own happiness. We have to be. When all some of us have known are heartache and loss, it becomes the help we needed when we were too young to know how to ask for it. This grief I carry is not yours, nor is yours mine. I will never act as if I now someone else's. I will never be that guy. But I will listen and hear you for who you are, for who no one else can understand, because for the better part of my life, no one was been able to do that for me. It is who I have been my entire life. If I am not self-sabotaging, someone is ultimately leaving me because of reasons having nothing to do with me. Life is such a cruel and unforgiving bitch, a true test of grit and character. I watched a podcast last night on YouTube with Shawn Ryan interviewing Mark "Oz" Geist, who was one of the GRS members in Benghazi during the September 11th attack that killed four Americans. He was speaking about hate in one segment and how he has dealt with it in his own life. Mark was one of several on the rooftop when three mortars impacted and killed two former Navy Seals. Mark sustained shrapnel wounds from the blast which almost cost him his left arm. He has had over twenty surgeries on that arm alone since then. His interview struck a chord with me as has each and every interview on Shawn's show. He spoke about religion and his own faith, which mine differs from most who believe in a single God. He is a strong follower of Christ. I will never judge anyone who is a believer. I hope no one judges me for not being that way. I do not give a fuck if they do or not. I have my reasons and they have their own. Mark gave his full reenactment of the situation that transpired over there. He also spoke about the movie "13 Hours" which depicted it for those of us who were not, to better understand the situation and aftermath of it all. To this day, no one has been indicted or charged with the actions that led to the terrorism and outcome of what happened. This world is eating itself in giant bites. It fucking sickens me to sit here and watch what is taking place in the United States, let alone all over the world. The politicians in charge are all pushing the grave it seems when it comes to their age. Tthe fact there is no age limit on the positions they hold, only means we will never get better as a country. For example, Nancy Pelosi is damn near eighty-four years old and running again for the senate. No one that age should be in charge of any decisions that will better us. For the record, I am neither Republican nor Democratic when it comes to politics. Joe Biden is eighty years old. He can barely stand up, speak, or think on his own. He is the puppet with a million strings tied to him. They are all being told what to do, say, and where to go. No president should be nearing nursing home status, sitting in an office of ultimate power, unable to think clearly. Mitch McConnell, is eighty-one years old and the Minority Leader of the Senate. He had an episode a few weeks ago where he had a stroke while standing at the podium. It is infuriating seeing these old-heads hold so much power and milking the government for every single dirty dollar they can make, legally and illegally. Crooked faces sit behind these seats of power, all who have their own agendas which do not serve the American people. I am thankful I do live in the United States because it allows its citizens freedom of speech. If I was somewhere else, I could never write a book like this. I say all of that to say this, to live in this world, you have to beat a cheating and lopsided system which empowers the elderly at the head of it all. There are no consequences for their actions. They may get a slap on the wrist here and there, but they go unpunished for crimes they commit on a daily fucking basis. At the end of their tenure, they get their pension and retire to some beach property to spend the millions they have sucked dry from the American tit, while the rest of us are barely making it and struggling to even pay bills and buy groceries. I can remember when I was a freshman in college. I had a diesel truck my father bought me. It was the first vehicle I ever had. I was two years late getting my license because of my home life, but my father wanted me to have something for college. He asked me what I wanted. I had no idea I was going to get it. I would have been just as happy with some beater, but he knew what I had gone through and wanted to be the father he always had been for us. The reason I wanted it, was because diesel at the time was cheaper than gas. It was one dollar and eighty-five cents back in 2004. I truly understand everything gradually goes up because of inflation and then resets itself to accommodate those of us living in this country. Sadly, nothing has leveled off in over a decade, or maybe closer to fifteen years. we were in a war for over twenty years and diesel never got over two dollars and fifty cents, until five to seven years ago. It is over four dollars for an average across the board. To live in this world, it means you must be willing to sacrifice. There was a survey done a few months back that said over seventy percent of Americans were maxing out their credit cards and living beyond their means. Another thirty plus percent were barely making enough to get by month to month. I do not ever preach on politics the government, or anything related to either of those, but ever since Covid hit, the world has changed for the worst. It will never go back to as it was before, but to see how everything is now has made a lot of us reconsider even living in this country. The price of oil per barrel is getting close to ninety dollars again. This year, price of fuel is even more expensive than it was this time last year. It is an absurdity and reckless on everyone's account who is in charge of this country's well being. People are dying by the thousands due to suicide daily. The average has almost doubled within the past year alone for males between the age of thirty and thirty-seven. I am living in a house that was built in the 70's. It is barely two thousand square feet, has three bedrooms, and two baths.

The foundation itself is atrocious. There is no insulation in the attic, which makes summer time a melting pot for those inside. There are cracks in the walls which allows the cold air of winter to get in whenever that season decides to show up. The summers are getting hotter by the year. The winters are in the same way getting colder. Monthly rent for this place is 1800 dollars, which is grotesque and ludicrous at best. The kitchen sink does not have hot water. The electrical outlets are a fire hazard and only half of those work. before we moved to Portland, we checked out another house that was built in 2006 on the other side of town. They were asking 1900 dollars a month for it. Looking back on it now, I am sure my father thought he was saving a hundred dollars, but in reality, he is wasting 1800 by living here. I do not and will not ever understand why he refuses to leave this hell-hole. I guess the older you get, you become illogically stuck in your own stubbornness. My younger brother and I have tried to get him to go to Utah, but he refuses to leave here if it is not for a trip to parts of the hill country. I will be forty in two years and I will not stay here and suffer because of his unwillingness to leave. My life needs to be lived to the fullest. I need to do what is best for me, and what is best for me now is to hold out a bit longer to make sure he is okay and hopefully get him out of here. that is the only reason I came back in the first place. To be here now, doing the same shit day in and day out has been the ultimate mind-fuck for me and my mental health. My happiness comes and goes. My good days come and go. My bad days follow suit. To feel as if you are eternally stuck somewhere you do not wish to be is and remains the ultimate killer of the soul. I urge anyone who feels trapped or suffocated by their life, to get out and travel. It does not have to be far away. it can be in a hotel in the next town or city over if you can afford it. Any place will do and is timely better than where you find yourself suffering and miserable. You will be surprised at what that can do to and for your psyche. Each time we go to Southlake for my dental appointments, you can vehemently tell the difference and feel the change it brings you. Being on the road alone gives me that.

I was not made to be settled down in one place. I did that in Utah because I was in love with the area. It was everything I needed from a place. I still got in my jeep and went places. I traveled up north to Salt Lake City to see my brother a few times. I went to Las Vegas, Arizona, New Mexico. If you are not taking advantage of the time you have, it will certainly take its advantage of you. Being stagnate only cripples your creativity. I constantly blow my own mind daily being able to write as much as I do here and continually finding new things to type about without ever going anywhere except the post office and grocery stores. There is nothing here except my father. If it were not for him, I would have never been here to begin with. I also know without him, I would not be here physically either in a lot of ways. I owe all of this to his patience and love, so I have tried to return that to him by being here for him. Maybe my brothers would have done the same if they were in my shoes and had the luxury of not having to work a real job, but I will never know because they never had to do what I am doing. I have been the custodian for both my mother and father at different points in my life. It is not something I would give to anyone else. It simply eats away at your growth and outlook on life. Though it does give you perspective in some ways, there is nothing but a set pattern to live by. The rules of which I have never followed nor have ever wanted to in the first place. There are only three months left in this year, then 2024 will be up next. I have no idea how the next three will go, but I do know I will be in Italy in less than three weeks with my father and younger brother. There is a promise in a trip of that magnitude. I will be packing two bags. One will have my typewriter and writing supplies. It will more than likely be the most I have ever been able to write before in a two week span, considering I wrote two books back in 2018 in less than two weeks. I cannot emphasize enough how much getting out of your comfort zone can save your life and turn you into the human you were destined to be. If you get anything out of this book, I hope you value your life more and worry less about who is not in it. Being a troubadour is more than just about writing and seeing the world differently.

It is about seeing yourself in a different light and welcoming in the change that proceeds it. We are all gifted at something. We are all put into this world for a reason. If you have yet to find your purpose, do not feel as if you have lost the chance to do so. it took me over thirty years to find this version of myself. I will not wait around another thirty to put all of my power into what it is I am after in the only lifetime we get. I will fall victim to a belief others have obscured. I will not allow my situation at hand to use and view me as prey it can feast upon. My bones are not ready to rest yet, nor is my mind for that matter. There is a soul within me, starving to be released again as I gave it power to five years ago. It will have its time. For now, I will use what power and control I do have to write about it and share all I can so the human who reads this can take back their own life before it is too late. To be able to do what I do for a living is a blessing I will never take for granted no matter how much I get used to it. There was a time when I had a service dog, drank all the time, and could not get out of my own head long enough to see that there was a way out. I have always had this gift within me. It took me becoming sober and dependent on myself to finally see it all through again. I am blessed by the gods to be able to see the world as I do, to have the family I have, and to have known love the way I have in this lifetime of seek and destroy. I am no better than the one reading this. I am simply a man of conviction when it comes to his scars and the wounds he carries. I am here to help as many as I can when it comes to finding new ways to gravitate towards their own path. my sobriety has been the most important part about my life and it will remain the most important thing I will ever do with my life. If anyone walks up to me and asks if I can help them with it, I will. If I can in any way produce a new sight and speech for someone to use as a way of guiding them where they want to be without being able to themselves, I will. The helper in me will never die. I believe I will be looking out for anyone who gets close to me. I know I will most likely look out for them better than I have done looking out for myself. Help anyone you can. It is our gift.

Chapter 10

-Poetry & Prose-

HEALER

you're finally free from everything. her smile turned into a widening half circle. "i am finally moving on from my scars. i have been free for a while, it just took me a little longer to accept what had happened and to know i needed life more than death needed me. i am not a quitter, but i wish i could've seen it through my windows sooner." there's this certain mystic thing about life when you abruptly find someone who at last appreciates your unfaltering passion and immoderate dedication for everything that is within you, making them so damn easy to love. it might seem unnatural at first because you never thought another could exist who shares your intake for life and love. i took the cape from my own heart it had been wearing and gave it to hers. it had been stitched on by using the stars from the universe's third eye. i need her to know how it feels to have something unbreakable for once. it happens too many damn times when people are born with an already brittle heart and never find someone who understands its cracks. i never knew i would have the capabilities to love someone so much, but with each beat, my entirety breathes for you. you picked me up by the bones and allowed me to stand tall once again. i no longer fall behind with dusk, on the other side of what could have been. you were the one who ignited the sky, creating a shimmer that withstood the breaking all over me, around me, and within me.

Cosmic Teachings

one time, someone told me, "there is nothing more than love." bullshit. love every day more than you did the last. love harder. love deeper. love as loud as you can. for the one you are with, they deserve your very best not just today, but the ones that make up an entire lifetime. you can always do more than just love. go beyond that. i am not trying to forget you dear. i am honestly trying to remember the life i had before you. before there was such a thing as you and i. i knew her before the universe understood who she was. she wasn't complicated. she was beautifully intertwined with a heart stained by stars, with a skillful mind that could always think for herself. after the chaos ensued and we learned what planets were, we would patiently sit on the moon and watch the earth, all the while wondering what life was like living amongst humans. always keep your head above the universe, sweet child. it is the only way you will remember how it feels to give hope to someone else who once thought they were dying of the missing pieces to their heart.

When Nature Is Your Religion

walking through this life, i've noticed how the trees maintain their balance with each new horizon my eyes have seen. they all seem to work as one, as they continue to grow from the same roots buried deep beneath the surface. though you cannot see it from where you are, below, they are teaching us how to survive and live this life together. life is made up of the known world we live in and the unknown reality that awaits us tomorrow. both can be daunting, but it also can provide us with a sense of wonderment if we allow it to.

The Escape

when i leave this place, i hope the carrying case for my soul is completely ravaged and bruised in all the places i have used to try and live with a fullness for a life without ever wondering, "what if." humans have a strange way of living. they are either too naive to think anything bad will happen or they are completely inept to handle life because they have had their hands held for them walking over the burning coals. i've always told people that i cannot wait to be old. the reason is simple. surviving, teaching, and showing others how to be yourself in all vulnerability is the best fucking part about living. i don't need you telling me what i have done right and wrong in this life. all i need from you is to understand the value of your words mean nothing to me if you cannot accept the fact we were all born to be our own dreams and wishes. i do not associate with those who are unwilling to chase the fire streaming down from the universe and forming the stars beneath your feet. i know i still walk on my clumsy hands at times, but it's only because i choose to actually feel the earth rotate when you cross my mind. she had this certain quality about her that made my soul break through the cage it was in. freedom for me was nothing more than being anywhere with her.

When No Extra Light Is Needed

the way she could take in a breath and breathe it out, made me believe she could bring back anyone who had been pretending to live. i thought of a life without you and that is when i began to believe those who had told me, "death is any form of existence without the one you love." i have started to drink more tea and less whiskey. i have started to listen to the older me more than the young and reckless soul i used to be. call me what you want, but i am living my life by heartbeats instead of heartaches. i put a lid on the bottle filled with demons and began sipping on her sweet sounds of immunity. my god, how fucking powerful it is to be able to live again without needing what was killing me for almost my entire life. i will always need less of this life around me and more of you every day. all she had to do was smile. whether i was looking or not, i could hear and feel it, but most of all i could hold it. it was as fresh as virgin skin, yet real enough to know i was not dreaming. it taught me that even the smallest of gestures can act as the foundation for the grandest of spectacles, knowing the phrase, "we are us," is such an awe-inspiring presence to be able to be around when two humans ultimately realize what life is truly about. learning what she tastes like during every savory dream i've had about her, allows me to wake up without needing more light to show me how close she is next to me. she smells like clouds that have just bloomed over the mountainous skyline, full of sage and purple rain.

In The Echoes Of Meaning

our love will continue to grow in the very dirt that takes me away. i shall hang onto the roots of each stellar attraction that has fallen just to grow closer to you and say your name each time another one falls from the sky of wishes. everything may die, but there is always a way to live for something far after you are gone. in-between each heartbeat of mine, my soul searches for new ways to love you more. it finds them in every kiss we share and every memory exchanged to save for another blissful time spent together, when nothing is left but to prepare for a new beginning. one thing will constantly remain the same, and that is no matter how much i can love you in this lifetime, i know how lucky i have been just to say your name out loud to the universe. you are the echoes made in this world and the next.

When Life Gives You Angels

my eyes focused again on her, "i have seen you before haven't i?" she looked around like most people do, not really sure if it is them being asked, "i do not think so. what's your name?" "my name is Walter, mam. i am sorry to have bothered you, but i swore you looked so familiar to me. i am sure you get that often." holding back her laughter, she smiled at me, showing all of her teeth. together and happily, it formed the most beautiful sight. "i know you. you are the woman who once lived in the shadows of her own tears. you used to live three houses down from me. your husband passed away from a heart attack a couple of months back. how have you been? the whole neighborhood has been looking for you." she started to walk away and then retraced her own steps to walk towards me. "i realized i was dying as well. i needed to not cry about what i cannot control. my husband was a loving man, with the strongest soul that ever existed, but time remains undefeated against us humans.

i decided to walk downtown today because i missed the morning birds singing and the strangers laughing. i missed who i was, but i know she died with my husband. now, i have been reborn, and if the only thing you do is roll out of bed this morning, never forget that in those few seconds, you will have accomplished a feat not everyone will be able to do. so when your feet touch the floor, stand up tall and fucking live this day for everything it is worth. too many of us do not get that opportunity to do such a simple task. the smallest of things we once took for granted at times, meant the world to someone else who cannot do them anymore. when there is no time to think, no space to fully live, allow the universe be your spotlight, your hand to hold. i would rather walk these streets admitting to those around me that i don't know a goddamn thing about this life, instead of running from place to place pretending i know how it feels to understand someone who sees the world through their mind rather than feeling each spot with their heart."

What We Become

i'll never forget walking through central park in july of last year. i noticed this little boy sitting on the wooden bench beside me. there were other parents around, and after a few hours i could tell none of them were his. i wondered what a child of his age was doing all alone during that time of day. i often went to the park to take in the sights and sounds of the world, then, out of nowhere, the little boy asked me, "excuse me sir. what time is it?" to my surprise and somewhat shocked that he wold even ask a question, i told him,"it is 5:41pm." the boy went back to his spot on the bench and proceeded to keep looking out into the open, as if he was desperately searching for someone or something. another thirty minutes passed and i tapped the young boy on his shoulder, "what are you doing out here all alone?" the boy took a moment to gather his thoughts and looked me dead in the eyes, and said, "i am not alone sir. i have been raised by the stars. the moon and sun watch over me. i am never alone, sir. i am a son of the universe and i am here now making sure you're okay. i know you, and i also know why you really come here. your wife passed away a year ago on this very day. she loved the park. the very one you used to despise before you met her. being here is now the only place that reminds you of her. please remember, you are never alone. even if the comely trees do not answer your questions and the stubborn ground stops moving for you, always come back to where you find peace. it's a special spot nobody else knows." i hope for the most part that i stay misunderstood. why be like those who are carbon copies of everything perfect in this world. i prefer to live a life dedicated to the strangeness happening around our bones than to be merely another voice in your head telling you i told you so. the boy left, and i was left with nothing but tears to remind me of his words. i know she is gone, but if i can find some sort of silver lining in this world, it is knowing she is still here, sitting with me on this bench, as i tell her everything i cannot tell anyone else now that she has left.

Where The Soul Goes

she finally started to love herself, and with that she stopped searching for the finer things in life. she understood that loving who she already was, would be the most priceless gift that one can receive. the only space needed for me is right between our colliding whispers. an explosion of anticipation unknown to those who have never had someone of her caliber. as we pulled into the driveway, i opened the door and grabbed her hand. we walked together through the rain and up to her front door. as i said goodnight, i kissed her cheek, and started back towards the truck. but my soul stayed behind to watch over her to make sure she would be alright. "to give your heart is one thing, but to give your soul for love is another. the two go hand in hand, just as we still walk together, holding onto everything we will ever need."

When The Dream Is You

i was tired today. it was a different kind of fatigue, as if my mind, body, and soul were all in the same place with you at once. i know when people say that when you cannot sleep, someone is dreaming about you. i believe that to be true. when i was as tired as i was today, you needed me more, and i gave everything i had to surround you and hold you with all of me. i understand it should be like that all of the time, but we are not flesh to flesh right now. i always know whenever you are in need of me, i will completely give all i have left in order to make you feel as safe and loved as you need. to provide and give you a type of comfort only i can accompany. maybe next time when you are drained from having your normal energy, it will be because of us being consumed by one another with a love we both need. you are that moment in time for me. as i sit comfortably on this bed of mine, i close my eyes to see all of the beautiful places we found last night.

Life Happens

i've walked the sandy shores of st. croix and swam next to buck island, while watching the travelers on the mainland scurry across the mountain side. i see one of the first childhood homes i grew up in when i lived in chandler, arizona. climbing the brick wall behind our house with my older brother to look out over the desert landscape. i miss those innocent days of being a kid, when the only worry on my mind was, "did i get dirty enough to have to wash my clothes?" if the answer was no, i had to discover new places in the yard so that being a kid made sense. i am the middle child, and i would always find myself in-between an argument amongst my brothers or in-between reality and a dream. i chose to be alone at times. not because i didn't have friends, but it made for a better world at times. i lived in new york and pennsylvania, yet my bones were not made to live in the cold. we made the best and most of it. wherever i was, i knew being inside the house was never for me. i felt like i was missing out on the universe and all that could be done while staying outside as long as i could. experiencing life as i did and understanding it as i now live today, there are a lot of lost memories. i know somewhere deep in my mind those days happened. what an amazing time it was. a child can be forever young, adventurous, and wise before the years turn into actually meaning something. life happens for them in all of the places you cannot see. the places adults can no longer envision. but that's reality for us all in a way. the child we used to be, still walks the halls of our souls, begging for a chance to one day play with the universe again. the one when being happy and free can be found by how dirty and filthy the clothes get from being audacious. here's to being everlastingly young at heart and fully in love, wildly in love with everything, because a mild love cannot start a fire. being wise about your circumstance and knowing the change that needs to take place before any new memories can be stored away for a reflection of youth is such an innocence lost. when i close these sun-struck eyes of mine, my vision is as clear as the day is new again.

Under Construction

my angels and demons threw me a going away party. they knew who you were, and you alone would always be all that i would ever need in this life. i apologize if i come off as someone who has been hurt before. the truth is, i have, and it nearly killed me. i don't want you to feel as if i can never love again. my heart has been through the fire and has come out still beating. i cannot thank you enough for reviving it after so many years of being in the dark. instead of burning alive, i am now burning for you. it is such a fucking glorious sight to see and to feel something alive actually burning for something again. it feels like everything was intended as i needed it to be with you. when beginning this, i was fairly certain you were not needing or wanting anything to do with me. when i think about a life i want to share with you, it all starts with me getting mine together finally. sharing a life with someone is the ultimate endgame for some, and it will be that way for me as soon as we help one another get there together. i know we already have a strong enough foundation for the framework to be started. i want to wake up each and every morning to the sound of your voice and the feeling of your whispers on my neck. i want a life that is assembled on friendship and trust. considering the love that comes with that, i know we can create anything. a life shared in my opinion consists of being happy, loved, and continually growing with each other and never settling for less than what is best for each other. we are more than just fading words on paper. we will always be the backbone to the structure of what we give life to. when i think about building a life with you, i know it will take both of our hands to put it together. i am willing and ready to love you until my last breath. i know we haven't met, but i honestly believe and know in my soul we were meant to meet in this life and become side by side humans, with souls fervent for each other. when i think about building a life i want to share, i think about your children, and how i can accommodate for them and help them grow as adults throughout the time we are together, helping them along their way and knowing that we will always be able to provide them with the help and guidance they need. i think about the kind of animals we will have and how much attention they will need when we are raising them. the location and house is still in the air, but i know in my heart we will find and make whatever we discover the most beautiful home there is for us. beach or no beach, you have touched a place in my heart and snatched a piece of my heart that had yet to be touched by a loving person. i know you have told me that you are nothing like me when it comes to those things, but together, i will never change you. i will touch you and love you in places you have never felt them before, allowing you to know my hands, body, and soul are rightfully yours. building a life together to me, means it takes more than one person, and there is no other person i would rather build it with than you. i know your circumstance and everything that is included, but i am here for you as i have said. i am not going anywhere. this is me. you can have me forever. i want to know what building a life is and what it takes only with you.

This Watch Is Ours

i will continue pursuing all of my aspirations in writing and whatever else that comes from my goals, but i know it will not always pay the bills. i am not that naive. i will search for the work that suits me and my capabilities, which will produce the money needed for us to have a life that we can always enjoy. in the same sense, we will both continue to work on it, because if you are not working at it, then there is nothing that you can get better at. i want to build a life out of what you and i could do and everything we have done so far. i need you. i remember you telling me one time that you thought i just wanted you, but the truth is, i need you, and i will always reach for you when i cannot sleep. when the moon isn't as bright as it should be, i will kiss you when the time is wrong and when the time is right. with us, there is no such thing as the right time. everything will be our time. done on our watch.

SEEKERS

maybe she was misunderstood. maybe she liked it that way, but we all have days when trying to understand others brings out the true test of our character. when deciding to help or ignore someone based on a perception, that is when we fail each other. continue learning from those who turn the other way at the things they view as different. they will be the ones who have already died inside with there heads buried in the sand, continuing to ask if life is nothing but digging another hole to view what being closed minded actually means. searching for answers in the earth when all you will ever need is in front of you, staring at you right in the soul. do not be like them. the world is already full of that kind of insanity. be gallant amongst the garbled negativity and bullshit you see on a daily basis. stand up and stand tall for those who need you. avoid and step over those who cannot see because of their own utter blindness.

Finding Yourself When Absence Finds You

there's a part of me that says i need to walk away from us, but there's another part that says keep fighting because everything we have is worth so much more than doubt. today, it hit me as i got out of bed, knowing things could be different now. i just wanted to sleep it all away and hope that i was only drowning in my dreams. life can be fucking discouraging and so damn overwhelming at times, then you find that subtle spot of sunshine and it warms and embraces you with everything you need. i think i will stay directly in the sun today, above the clouds since it has been raining here since the early hours. i will find what i need there and then i will make a decision on what i need to do. unless you already know the answer and want to tell me, then please, go ahead and do so. i am old enough to take the truth and live my life if i have to without you. this is so goddamn hard to write. i am literally shaking. anxiety is creeping up beside me and i can feel it coming on, but breathing for as long as i have in the wreckage that had once been my life, i know i can and i will survive today because you taught me how to be alive again. how words and actions actually mean something when they are placed together. how getting up off the floor takes all of your effort and not just half-assing your way through it all. how a single good morning and goodnight can bloom life inside the soil of your soul. if this is the end, i know i was all i could be for you. i know i did all i could have for you, for us. i was not the one who left. i was not the one who made me think i was the reason again for the millionth time in my life. i should have let go of you sooner. i did not have the will or ability to after everything you had told me, because this kind of rock-bottom love makes us all sick and loony, attempting to restore a human who was using you all along for your own energy and space. you did not leave me empty handed tough. you taught me how much of me is still left and able to fight for his own life. you taught me how i never needed anyone else. i needed to trust myself again for the first time since i was on my own before i met you.

When Remembering Becomes A Grave

the feeling of being loved over and over again will sometimes be just as cruel as putting your heart to an open flame, burning and searing it with an endless amount of pain trying to scar it enough to where there is no more room for others to torture it. trying to kill off the love inside of you, will only make your time here shorter. make sure you can live with that the next time someone you love who cannot love you back, because of what you already did to yourself. i will meet you in california, and there you will find your name drawn in the sand by the fingers on my left hand. for when the time comes, that side of my body will be yours. it has always been us. it just took me longer to find my better half. i never thought life would get in the way so many times, but i guess it got in-between things i did not need and lead me to the thing i would always need. that is you, darling. your love. your kisses. you being you will always be more than i could have ever dreamt about. i have thought about finding you, but i could never see beyond the clouds following me, until you broke through all of it. you shined on me, and i caught your love in my heart. it is the biggest dreamcatcher i know of. i cannot tell you how lucky i feel to have met you. i am not sure if it was fate or superior timing, but what i do know is that my life will never be the same. i will forever be happy with its purpose. it was a bet and i pushed all of my chips in. now i know you. whatever words exist in this world and whatever book they are resting in, they will never be up to the task when it comes to trying to describe your love. it is something i have never felt in my entire life. it is a bond. one of which will never leave me. i once told you that when i let go, i let go completely. that is a lie. i hope i never have to. even if i do, i will never be able to let go of your hand. the same hand that led me to this point in my life. the one that is soft as sunday. the one where my heart loves to sleep. you have allowed me this chance. no matter what you tell me or think, it has always been you. it will always be you. whoever reads this, i am in love with her. the gypsy blood that runs through her soul. the extraordinary freedom that makes up her bones. the taste of forever laced on her lips. a touch of a thousand angels. this is a love i have never known, and to think, i was only lucky at first. my love, i am truly honored to have you in my life. goodnight and sleep well knowing i will see you soon when our eyes are closed. when they close, the rest once lost will return to me. it will all be dressed in your colors and softness. i am sure others have tried to love you, or at least show you how much they did. you gave me an opportunity to hold you. i will never take that for granted. what we had will never be had again. i know when you lay your head down on your pillow tonight, you will think of me, even without me there by your side. you will wonder for the rest of your life what might have been if you had stayed. i cannot and will not give your name solace and shelter within these pages i write anymore. i cannot continue going back to your grave and share with you how much i miss you. missing only leads us to a remembrance. something i no longer have the heart for.

Highway Robbery

do you remember the piece of me you stole? i hope it burns in your hands tonight. the one i love now and will forever love, replaced it with her love and reshaped my heart to fit my soul. she loved something more than who i thought i was. she loved someone who was incomplete. all of these years, if it has taught me something, it is this, to love is one thing, but to be loved by someone who opens their scars to bleed with yours, that is forever. happiness to me is something i have searched my whole life for. people have told me it can be anything you want it to be. i never listened to them until i met you. it's not that i didn't believe in the word. i was merely waiting for my heart and soul to align and agree, so i would know for sure what it is supposed to feel like. now, i do.

To The Lonely, It Does Get Better

i wanted to hear a story, so i went to watch the splintered park benches bleed the words that had been saved from the souls who had no one to talk to. now i know of a life by itself, but the truly lonely ones who wander this place in the twilight hours when all eyes and ears are closed, they are the ones who know how it feels to be death's comfort and closure. it has always amazed me how you built a home from a heart, soul, and bones. you have not only been the beginning to me, you are everything that will end with me. it is the most beautiful form of living i could have ever wished for. with a morning sun for a heart, i am alive when it breaks the horizon. one that will only beat to the sound of your soul as you carry my love on the inside of the notes it plays for you. i wanted you to become free, because you were not born to be anything else but a woman full of loving madness.

Self-Made

i remember the time you once wore chains around your wrists. they were placed neatly behind you, as if you were just another normal creature. now, you have used those chains as collars for the world and the end of the leash is in your hands. you control the gravity of which those around you spin. i sincerely hope they understand you are not one who will ever relinquish the power just so that you can fit in. keep creating your own universe in such a way, that when you breathe, those around you will be able to feel just how powerful the eye of your own storm can be. do not fear the beauty of finally letting go. for when you do, the rains that had once drowned you, will suddenly turn into bridges and gateways for the other parts of your heart that had once been under water. dry off the tears it had once cried and put on your favorite song. have a glass or two of wine, put your feet up on the stars and relax. you are where you need to be. you, my dear, you have made it your own.

Victories Of Life

even when my hands and arms are weak and sensing defeat, they will never be lowered to the level of which this world is trying to push them to go. they might get tired at times from holding up my own mind, but what i think and mean, will always be how i truly feel. there is no such thing as giving in. there is only pushing forward and raising the level of your awareness for those around you. always search and find answers that have been buried deep beneath the hardened surfaces below your eyes. climb the fucking mountains no one else will dare travel up because the view from the peak is not what they want you to see. climb, crawl, dig, fucking break through anything holding you back. be stronger than those who are willing to stand with the faceless crowd and make your own company sweeter than ever. even if it is just you, at least you know where you stand when the fight takes on more of your time. those who were once broke and looking for unconditional love, continuing to scrap with life willing to sacrifice their heart for another who is in need of a place to stay. battle for as long as it takes. do not surrender all of your progress to be told, no. you are in control of it all. every decision. every action. all of it. you owe yourself the best opportunity at this life. i hope you never give up a single day of your life because someone tells you it is not worth it. no one could be more fucking wrong and naive to what is going on in this world. the hope we all need is within the very day we are living. it is how we know who we are and what we are doing matters. as long as you have it, no one will be able to take it away from you. we are the victors. we are the kings and queens. we decide our fate by the path we take. the blood and misery we have been through, was only a testament to the heroes we are for our own lives. if you are to do anything with your life, make someone else feel as if they matter in their own. i believe it is the truest sign of being a human. something you once forgot how to do because of the ones in your circle, will become second nature again once you figure out what they are doing will only shrink your soul.

Left On Repeat

sitting here, watching the people come and go. leaving the ones they love for another trip into the unknown. as i used the phone it seemed like my heart was beating out of my chest. with all the butterflies you give me, i still get nervous. leaving behind what seems like a million lifetimes, it's going to be unlike any other goodbye. i can see you in front of me but i see you everywhere. in the morning, i will be leaving. in the months to come, it is you i will be needing. pain is temporary. heartache is forever. now, i only miss you when i wake up. everything in life has it's own expiration date. don't be spoiled. enjoy this life for what it is. why say anything at all to me, when saying anything hurts the same. one of these days, i will find someone who is willing to help me unpack my baggage, instead of adding more to a packed bag. i have been waiting by the phone for so long, everything is gone. You know it is something special when you feel your soul moved. you gave me a reason to smile again. if i could relive only one day of my life, for the rest of my life, it would be the day i met you.

Railroad Runaway

i loved you, and maybe it is over, but in a million different ways, it will never be. i know with certainty and a delicate sensation, i loved you more than any human is allowed to almost give their own life for. for me to be able to say that, not only internally, but externally to someone else who may wish to want me close to them, is an invaluable and heartbreaking realization i will never be enough for them and they will never be, you. allow me to dissipate in my solitude, to simply disassociate who i am from the stories you have heard about me. i am not looking for anything or anyone. i am sitting with a stillness only appreciated by those who have been running away from things they will never fucking outrun in this life.

Slow Down, Dear Child

we have ran far enough. our wings can only take so much earth until they become staged beside the graves we will become once our lungs become blackened by the dead dreams we carry. lean into the breath you have been saving for grace and redemption. there is nothing greater in this life than overcoming the state of fear and filling your eyes full of the wonders of this world. stay steady and all time ready for what is about to take place. the face you see today will change. it is all about the story and these scars we wear so proudly that will keep our heads above the framed outlook of defeat. love is real, because you once said it to me when no one else had the courage to.

Prize Fighter

you had the sweetest first breath of anyone i had ever met. i know i was not the first to feel it or know of its powers. i know the candles must have felt its innocence each and every time you made your wish. years have gone by now since then, and you have become a mother, a queen, and a darling wonderling. you are the exact feeling and presence everyone needs, but rarely gets to know. you do not deserve to have blood on you that is not yours, but you have been cleaning up anything with a pulse before the moon was even born. after all you have been through, your heart is still beating and beautiful. may we all know those who fight for us when our fight becomes lost. i know with a certainty that something beyond love keeps you in my life, and i can only hope at the end of my dog days, anyone who has read my books, knows your name and how immortal it is.

BUTTERFLY

you were never one to have long nails because of your love for playing in the earth and making sure your flowers had your presence and love with them. you cut your own hair because you are intimidated by the beauty salons more so than any doctor office, which i find endearing. you tend to wear the same three or four outfits, walk barefoot, and tend to your gardens. a true moon walker of sorts, you are. you never say it out loud, but part of you is envious of women who always look pretty and well-kept, in your own words. you do not care for it at all, which makes you one with yourself as a quiet dream, day-walking around those who need everything perfect to feel perfect, to feel seen and royal in a lot of ways. your unruly curly hair and tomboy demeanor gives off an image of some little girl still playing outside while the rest of the world is sound asleep. all freckles and curious, you once ran on beaches, chased crabs until dinner, and climbed every tree that told you, you never would. you collected matchbox cars, star wars figures until you were a teenager. you were in love with your huffy, watched raiders of the lost ark at least a hundred times, and could throw a ball a mile. you jumped from cliffs, and now you barely step near them. fear may have you now, but i see you as the woman i want to jump each one of them with.

A Child Deserves More

as a child, just as i was old enough to realize what happiness was, everything changed. people still ask me today why i am afraid of it. i have known sadness to be a friend, something that will not judge me for not being how others appear to be on the outside. on the inside, i am still crying about what i lost on the day happiness found me. i am still on my bedroom floor, wondering what i did to deserve the home i grew up in and the family that never existed. my happiness is not dependent on someone's understanding of it. it is me believing in it enough to allow myself to. i have worked my entire life to heal my inner child. i can tell this year will be the time i actually do. do not neglect yourself anymore. you deserve someone who wants to help you through it, even if you are scared out of your fucking mind to give in and allow someone to be who you never had growing up. it is time for a proper mourning. it is time to move on for good.

Holding More Than Flowers

i have been in your head before. i know how silence tastes once it has grown old. i know how lonely it feels when your bones decide to leave you. i know what love sounds like once you have abandoned your own life. i know all of it too fucking well. it still knows my name, but it does not know my life. we are not our darkness. we can at times be our own light. at the end of it all, we are simply doing our best to have a memory or a few to hold onto and keep with us before it all goes.

<u>*ROME*</u>

to me, you have always been the moon and earth breathing. a simple truth for the wicked, a subtle response for those needing to be heard. i crossed my heart the day i met you. a pinky promise to the lies i had been led to believe in, died the same night i held you as if you were the last living thing to believe in its own beauty. if rome was our song, you were the entire city, cathedrals, religion, and all of the art creating muses for those in need. if you do go before i do, i will lay next to the earth where you are, while you keep what is underneath me warm. i may have been made to be alone, but that was before meeting you. now, i cannot even wish these days away since you have been gone. i miss you is a weak attempt at describing how i feel, so wrote this instead.

The Bridges We Become

i am the one you date if you want to marry after me. i do not know if it is a curse not to find love when it is all you are after or if there is such a thing as giving up right before you reach it. i am happy for you. i am happy you found someone who told you what you needed to hear, who made you believe staying was something that could be done when all you did your entire life was run away from yourself. i was going to ask for your hand a few months back, but life stopped for both of us in a lot of ways neither one of us saw coming. i know we all find out what happens when whatever does happen is meant to be. at least now i know happy knows you better than how sadness once held you. i have written hundreds of letters hoping you would get to read them. i will use them in a book and then burn them, one by one. some of us are the bridges for others to find their unification of soul and body. i am okay being that if it means i get to torch the last one, then build a road over it so i can drive and meet someone halfway, instead of us both jumping in to save the other from an early death of hope.

The Secret Places We Hide In

you have overcome so much in your life. the abuse you never speak about. the lonely times when you contemplated dying and wondering if anyone would miss you. the days when you could not get out of bed because all of the gravity forcing you to stay under the covers felt more like protection than punishment. you knew it could not go on forever with the way you hated yourself for not being able to say, no. for always saying, yes, more times than you needed to. you have looked at everyone you have ever loved with dead eyes, but a spark only a handful recognized. you have held your breath under water to see how far your could get until you gave in and found your will to breathe again. there are journals you have kept hidden in the sidewall of the second drawer no one knows are there. one day, you will finish the last one with words about love for your own life, without adding an unnecessary goodbye not even you would believe in enough to write.

It Was All My Fault

i wish i could have told you how you were not the only one hurting, but what man compares his own scars to the ones that live visibly inside of the woman he loves. i wish i could have told you how some days the light alone makes my entire body ache from loneliness not caused by you, but from the days of having nothing to hold onto except for its warmth. i wish i could have told you how heavy the world gets for me when you can barely move to rearrange your insides long enough to keep starvation from eating the last good parts of you. i know you were constantly dealing with a ghostly and neglected childhood that made you who you are today, and how much of it continues keeping you from being able to love and trust as you once did before you had your heart fucking broken the first time by your father. i could, and vehemently tried my very best to relate, because mine was broken by my mother and then again by my father when he left. i went to sleep that night in love with you and woke up afraid for my life. it had nothing to do with you. we are still children trying to forgive ourselves for not being there when we needed more than love to save us, hold us, protect us.

Who You Are For Your Own Life

life will not be like this forever. we give and take just as life and death taught us at an early age. your purpose is beyond what others have shown to you, given to you, and told you what it was meant for. your heart is the most important part of your journey. feed it, listen to it, and when you need to, grieve with it. the worst thing we can do is waste an entire lifetime pretending we are okay, when we know what is hurting is not always ours to blame. you may not be where you want to be right now. you may not have everything you thought you would have by now, but this path you are on needs you. this day is not a reflection of who you are not. it is a stepping stone into becoming your true-self once and for all. blessed are those who walk when staying down feels better on the bones. you must not forget, we are everyone we have ever met, every place we have been, and the human we have always required. may our colors run wild throughout the sky and fill up every ocean running dry and empty. you are the moon's favorite child, a friend to every blinding sun, and a warrior's representation of a battle won.

Love Is A Helper's Rendition

fall into me as many times as you need to. i can take it, i promise. i have been hardened by this world ever since my mother turned me away and replaced her love for me with the hate she had kept with her from her own life. it is where i get my darkness from, but it is the same place where my love exists. lean into me as many times as it takes for your back to release its hunch and the burdens you have been carrying ever since you were told nothing you do will ever suffice. bring your fears to me. whether it is one or a thousand of them. we will burn them together and watch the ashes take form of an entirely different human. from here, you will take your first strides again, as a warrior, as bravery itself. i will see the devil leave your eyes, just as you will see him leave mine. in this life, we do not always find a love that stays, but we do find helpers along the way who turn out to be the next best thing. fall into me. i will show you how to rise and stand once more on a piece of earth no one ever took time to show you had been yours all along.

For All The Moons

you are an unremarkable act of glistening defiance. something inside of you never died as you grew older and the world became a bitter place for lovers and keepers of a certain youth. you always had the ability to preserve the light in every room you walked into. you always made the doorway look taller than it was. your hands were not made for letting go. your eyes were not made to be shaded by a sun and moon destined to fight lifetimes to find a common bond amongst the hazel hues colored around your memories. i began to realize quite quickly into discovering you, how rare it was to have someone compliment you for a past you almost died in. i knew if my stories could not make you leave, maybe these scars would be able to scare you and break you away from me. but nothing ever came from it bedsides an evergreen smile being shown to me by another human. i never dreamt of an act like you finding me without killing what was left of my attempts to show courage by smiling back. i had not known happiness in over a decade. my burdens were the only ones present at my table when i would eat the scraps i was being forced to digest. i have often wondered what life would be like if i finally removed you from it. it does not scare me, but it does remind me how few humans i actually have in my circle who know me, who know the relevance of the dead i sleep with to keep anything living from getting closer than i am comfortable with. one day, someone will ask me to tell my story again for the thousandth time, to begin telling it from where i found myself before anyone else had found me. i will have to measure out the cost of explaining to them how each chapter of my life has to deal with a woman i loved greater than anyone before her. you are an oak tree that i will never be able to chop down, even if i am asked to. no bonfire deserves to have you inside of its flames. you have already made magic out of the ashes before. your supreme mentality and quick wit made me crave you from the very first time you opened that sweet mouth of yours. everything else about you was a representation of how long you had survived by being who you needed when change was called for. i may go to my final resting place never immersing myself within the every moon you once collected for me. but i do know a sun can survive without the light given off from other celestial creatures. if goodbye finds us, please know i tried my fucking best to love you more than anyone you had ever given that chance to. there was a promise we spoke about. the one where you would always keep my hand in yours, regardless of whomever found you after me. i know you still love me, and maybe you always will. when my hand becomes clenched for no reason other than me feeling your hands, i will know you kept your word, your promise, and bond to me to forever feel me as i will for you.

Naked Truth

perhaps i was too young, too permanently construed, but i knew if i were to love you, there would be no coming back from it. i lifted you as high as i could, beyond moons, beyond infinite truths. i sought you out, like a tin-man torn apart by war looking for someone to restore his heart and kiss his face slowly, full of golden and silver offerings. come to me, with an embrace wide open and eyes that never blink before love is made. lay down with me, naked as the dawn before summer cheats on winter with autumn's breeze. i know i will not be able to have you fully in this life because your soul is loved by another. letting go is all i can do in order to survive the next winter without you. you and i found every rainbow we could, but our luck died, and now, i have every color that is not you staring back at me after the rain has left me, too.

Blood. Guts. And Royalty

there will never be another you, so take love with you wherever you go whenever you can. your heart belongs to you and to those you have allowed to know just how giving and gentle it has always been. when others speak of royalty, they mention your name, your face, the way the gods sculpted your soul from lightning. never forget your power, your braveness, and just how far you have had to go to run into yourself where you are today. the obscured path is not for everyone, and that is why we mistake lonely for love. that is why we constantly find ourselves on the outside looking in most of the time. where we are going, those of us who have known struggle, failure, and setback in an intimate way, we will be a place for all kinds. you are the backbone of the constellations. you must not let yourself ponder about who it is you see in the mirror, in the eyes of those who barely know you. you are the gilded crown, the cape, and momentum of gravity.

Imperial Summers

you move as if you have never shied away from life at all, even as it was taking more away from you than you had left to give. a perfectly placed smile for the imperfections of what others believe it to be, when all we are, are paintbrushes and typewriters, trying to create a better life to be a part of. i have stared out of these same windows for almost four years now. i have often thought about how caged i was until i saw the sun playing with the trees and flowers where they have been and stayed now for an entire lifetime before my thoughts and i showed up. i could write about anything and find love and joy because of it, but i have found more blood and reason to believe there is more left on these grizzled bones to live for. you have become my journal, or possibly the other way around. however missing someone actually works is still a mystery to me. i have missed you since i asked the heavens for someone to see me and assist with my suffering. i saw your flowery face in the moon, and i never thought i would be able to get to you. but here you are, all light and luna, wrapped in whispered flesh.

Grit & Grace

i have watched you grow for a while now, from seed to earth, from ray to sun, from child to someone's reason to believe in humans becoming miracles. you were nothing but grit and grace in the beginning, a shy smile hiding an old soul beneath it all. over the years, you have outgrown your skin, your anxieties, your fears, and anything anyone told you to be weary of. a heart like yours should never hear the sound of its own breaking, of it shattering for someone who has never looked at you and saw themselves at ninety and you not being there to tell their best and worst to. you may be all fire and wild, with wings spread over the ocean's deep blue, but you are all orange and red when it comes to finding what is yours. a lighthouse for the sun and moon, you have transformed flesh and bone into meaning something beyond what this world once told you, you were. today, you are nashville and country, sunglasses and poetry being read somewhere near Marrowbone Lake. you are the love of your own life, and that is why you are your mother's child. cherish the beauty around you, but never forget your own. this town is yours to build. this world is awaiting to be yours all over again.

ARDOR

i am still here. though death has known my name and has greeted me a few times, my purpose still breathes. my fire still welcomes the earth. my air is still next to me. my scars are still my friends. my depression rarely checks in. my anxiety sleeps most days. my alcoholism rests comfortably at my feet, never asking for a drink. my chest gets heavy, but the pain reminds me i am here. i still have a chance to make a fucking difference in this world. that is what this entire life revolves around in my opinion. no matter how you feel or what has been done to you, you are still here. that specific belief alone is a beautiful sentiment and feeling to share with others who ache for a little more madness to kiss them on the lips, and say, it is okay. you are still here.

Seasonal Differences

we are settling for partial and disconnected love just so that we have someone to rid us of our lonely. i find it terribly bittersweet and fucking distasteful. if you are that desperate, learn more from what is around you, instead of what is not in your life currently. absence brings comprehensibility. though it, too, is a liar sometimes, it may make you think you need a warm body to be at peace, but the warmth depends on the love. absence is not a finished product until you take back your hands that have been in a begging position, clinging onto another seasonal happening. spring remains loyally at your side, blooming and sharing its own residual warmth collected from every summer that has been without you to contest for it.

Before A Moon Goes Blue

you will be 222,043.27 miles away from here tonight, and today feels to me as if you have never been closer. you will be the biggest and brightest full moon of the year, a true wondering and empowering blue moon. i have been tied to you since the beginning, with one end of the red string around your pinky and the other around mine. i can remember as a kid when i would make a telephone out of string and two cans. to this day, i swear you were on the other end. but i know if i told you, i love you, then wrote it out in my blood, you would tell me i am not giving enough, that what i am after will never be for us. i will look up to see you as you have always been her way home, her passing of light through human's eyes. you have your life now and i have mine, a paused emotion full of held back and revoked depictions carved out of a broken state of mind. i will keep everything at a distance, because that is what happens to those who get their soul stolen before the body knows it is gone and missing. before the moon turns blue, this broken mind will rest again.

I Am Not A Role Model

there is never a warning when it comes to loving who you find at the end of a rope you and your neck are hanging by in order to keep yourself from feeling what you could not correct. every love does not feel the same, but lucky for me, she caught me before the chair moved beneath my feet and kept my body and love from becoming another lifeless display of what not to do when you are not yourself in an argument between a devil and ghost, between barely and almost.

The Replacements

i still wonder about you and if you made it back up on your feet gain after caving in with all the thoughts you told no one about. i know the day is too long for some and the nights never give us the right song to listen to when our minds are full on what could have been. you have always been a gentle sleeper, but you have not been sleeping in over a year. you toss and turn yourself out of bed and onto the floor, as if your body rejects comfort of any kind. i know how that feels. i have been there for a while now myself, looking up into the darkness where your ghost loves to stalk me. i remember watching you and seeing how you could never stand still, even when there was nothing else to do but rest. you are not made for the subtle parts of life or the calm seas of paradise. it is either heaven or hell for you with anything you do. we met somewhere in the middle of those worlds, and now i search for you in movies, books, and anything to remind myself you are out there, still as restless as i am for the things we love. i hope wherever you find yourself today, the sun is shining and the moon lays down with you to ease your troubled mind. i hope you found something to replace me just as i was forced to do with you.

Buon Compleanno

i am thirty-eight today. i do not know what i did to deserve the life i have now where i can write for a living and still find time to take care of my own needs. my dad asked me this morning if i feel any older. i told him i actually feel better than i did this time last year. i know my body does not always concur with my mindset. i still feel young to have lived the life i have up until this day. i got up at six this morning to go run six miles, then workout when i got back. i am drinking my second cup of coffee now, waiting on College Gameday to begin in an hour. i bought myself four red velvet cupcakes and some candles so i can make my wish and give the last two cupcakes to my father. i did not buy myself anything else and will enjoy another year of life, of football, and another year with family and friends. when i tell people my life is simple, that is what i mean. i would be just as happy and content sitting somewhere in the forgotten space of humanity, being able to sip my coffee and watch the birds sing the sun up. thank you all for this past year. i hope all is as it should be for you. i could go on and on about today, but my mental health is good, my smile is obnoxious, my heart is less heavy, and for the first time in my life, i actually believe it will all be okay. everything is better when you are up with the moon before the humans wake up, before they know your real age.

Fools Rushing In

i get so tired of living, but i carry on with a promise i made myself to battle and survive by any means necessary, with rage or deep breaths. once you find yourself crossing over into the darkest parts of yourself, the only light you find is the kind you had to burn in order to stay alive. anything i do will never be enough for most, and when it is, it will not be enough for myself. we all live in a peculiar world, a resentful and perpetually uneven one where others believe it to be different than what it really is. we are in a simulation that never equally shares its grace amongst its recipients. someone is on the dying side. another is on the other side of living. all of life is cyclical. we are fools to think an ending can be where it all stops.

In A Lover's Knot

there you are, all showing and suffocating my sweetest thought. these teeth need a piece of you. any part will do, as long as you tell, yes, in the way you do. i know these words do not mean as much as i would hope for them to, but it is the only conversation i can place onto paper that you can be a part of right now. where you are in life is not where you would prefer to be, because there is no freedom, no joy in having the wind play with your hair as it once did, back when you were thirteen going on twenty-one. i wish i could snap my fingers and change both of our lives, or at least make being with you more of a reality than sleeping without you by my side. i know we would not waste a single day or thought, because once two souls touch, there is no coming apart. you are as much of my life as these hands typing out every last word for you to read, hoping you can draw independence and inspiration from them the same way i watch you breathe. i wish you never had tears in your eyes like you did last night. missing you is like missing a life i never had, but i would still know and feel you as if i had loved and touched you every fucking minute we spent tied and twisted in a lover's knot.

Playing With Paper

remember who you are and never forget it. we walk the line full of fire and falsehood, the only truth we know, is we create our hope. i will never know your pain or what you endure on a daily basis. but there is an understanding of souls, and i know relating to someone on that level is the therapy we all need from time to time. if you ever need to, take this day, fold it as neatly as you can into the paper airplane you need. you can throw it as far as you want to. i am simply here wishing a safe landing finds you.

Truth From Fiction

i was just writing dreams until you showed up.
i have been entirely consumed by you, and now,
i have forgotten how to die. i once wrote words
to merely survive, but you are the reason for
them today. you are the reason for a lot of
things taking place and changing right in
front of these autumn eyes.

COMELY

you are nestled right behind my eyes. what i see, you see. what i feel, you feel. a connection of energy without slack or tension, a layered emotion without turning back. i thought i lost myself until you showed up, until you brought everything i had gave up looking for again. i know nothing except for tomorrow, it will all be true again. each and every word placed between a brokenness and forged breath.

When It Becomes Defined

i am still trying to attach my fingers back to my hand, my heart back to my soul. i am a walking question, an unmatched emotion. my brain is quick to leave with any love showed and given to it. it is hard to be who you are supposed to be when every part of you that you once loved is with someone else. but i am reeling it in slowly. i have been taught by many, it is not the death of a love that defines you. it is how many times after it all fails for you that you discover a thankfulness for the flowers laid at your feet when we are ready to move on again. each petal becomes a savored breath for your roots to sink their teeth into.

The Laugh That Changed The World

i told you that this was my last attempt at love. and then you left me as if i was not good enough after all. may we all find the love we have dreamt about, felt profoundly within the emptied corridors of bones and soul. may we never be without a truth which surrenders the fear of being alone. we are and remain human, because we have never just been the broken pieces. we are the laugh after it all comes together for us when we least expect it to.

Chapter 11

-The Ending-

The last four weeks have been such a whirlwind of emotions. I have not worked on this book since the middle of September. I have taken a vacation of a lifetime, which I will not get into with this book, but I hope you take time for yourself. I hope you find time for yourself. It is paramount we find a way to disconnect for a while from this place, from the entire social media world. It was causing me immense anxiety and depression, along with other distractions that were taking me away from what I needed to be doing. I allowed other people's posts and photos to dictate how I felt and went about my own life, wishing I was someone else for a while. It has been a hell of a journey for me with the writing I have been working on since 2014. This was the first true vacation I have had since then and the longest I have been away from working. I know a lot of us cannot afford to do that. I definitely could not have afforded it on my own if it were not for my younger brother doing the majority of the work and planning. Life here in the States is such a rat-race, a workaholic's pleasure room. If you are not constantly finding new ways to survive here, you will not make it. I honestly do not know how families are making it work these days. With inflation making prices for everything astronomical, it is nearly impossible to make it work unless you are maxing out three or four credit cards in the process. I have found a new gear for myself since returning. It is not as massive or diluted as it once was for me. Even though my social media pages have been suffering because of my lack of posting, I now know I cannot keep doing what I had been doing prior to me being back. I miss traveling. I miss getting in my car and taking road trips. Gas prices have gone below three dollars for the first time in almost a year here. I know it will not last forever, but it is strange and depressing to feel happy about $2.77 fuel prices after experiencing a time when it was hardly ever over two dollars. The new norm is inescapable for the lower and middle classes as I am in. I read an article recently that said even if you are bringing in $250,000 dollars a year, you are barely getting by, even with the help of credit cards and loans. Pressing beyond your means is the quickest way to be in debt for the rest of your life. Just ask my father how that has worked out for him. It has been troubling to say the least since he lost job in 2018 and barely getting enough social security to pay the bills. I wish I had found a way to study the markets better or was taught how to invest properly. I know I could have had more money than I do now, but such is life when it comes to figuring it out on your own. The weather has finally changed here. This part of Texas had its first cold front the day we left for the trip. It has been moderately cool the last few days here, sunny and blue skies, with temperatures in the upper 80s and lower nineties. October is more than halfway through now. Halloween will be here in a few weeks, then November will bring families together for the first true holiday of the year with Thanksgiving. I always look forward to this time of year, because of Fall being my favorite season. It will be nice to spend some quality time with family and see how they all have been this year. I am still exhausting my options of finding a new life by the beginning of the new year. Being honest with myself, I still feel stuck here, a true suffocation of both mind and heart. I do not know when I will able to leave for good with my father being without a vehicle or a means of taking care of himself. It saddens me to see the state my father is in after living a life full of greatness and wealth in a lot of ways. We never had rich money, but we did at one point have enough money to do everything we wanted to do and he had more than enough money to spoil us as kids. I hope one day to be able to do the same for him, even after taking him on this trip to Italy, I still want to do more for him. My dream would be finding a new home for him and making sure he never had to pay another bill for the rest of his life. I have checked to see how much money you are supposed to have saved by certain ages. I am on track to having the average it says a thirty-eight year old is supposed to have by now. There is more for me to do in the future and more projects I will be doing. I also know I could get a side job at any given point to help facilitate whatever it is I am after and whatever it is I want to do in this life. I never had an ending number of pages for this book to consist of. I wanted to write as much as I could until I felt satisfied with the project and unleashing it into the world. One more baby for me to care for out in the world is how I view my books. Children I will never have, but I will always love and adore the projects I am able to create and share with the world. I thought I had someone I could have loved who basically ignored all of my words and feelings a few months ago. It was not new to me. I suppose when you write for a living, not a lot of people will take you at your word when you express yourself to them in a way they have read your words before. I wish it were easier to find simple love, to discover companionship in these times. The world is imploding with wars breaking out all over the Middle East and Europe. It feels as though world war three is upon us and closing in faster than any of us saw the world becoming before 2020 arrived. It all seemed and felt like simpler times. I honestly cannot remember life that well before the pandemic hit us. The world stopped for almost a year and left many of us behind. The rich got richer and the poor lost whatever we had left, in wealth and people. I am doing my best to make life work for me these days, all the while constantly thinking about my father and how to get him out of here. To be my age, you never think you will have to take care of anyone that is not your significant other. I remember my mother living with her parents in the house they moved into when she was a teenager. Being that close to a situation you did not fully understand ultimately prepares you for a similar life should it ever find you. My older brother has his family. My younger brother has his life, and travels too much to be able to help more than he already does now. I am the middle child. I have been a fucking custodian before I was even ten years old, looking after my mother, and making sure she would not lose her mind on my younger brother and myself. All the way until now, I am doing all I can to make sure my father lives to see at least eighty years old. Not complaining is something I am extremely good at, but when it comes to journaling and getting these decaying thoughts out so they do not implode and die within me is an everyday process. Trying to save money, while helping out with groceries and bills is an entirely different issue I deal with on a constant basis. Thankfully, I have been able to save up enough for me to get out of here, but there is still not a way for me to do that at this moment. All I can do is my best, which is me writing, creating books, and working out, attempting to stay as healthy as possibly both mentally and physically. We are not good to or for anyone if we are not sound minded and physically able to do what we need to throughout our days here on earth. The downside with me being away for as long as I have, are my book sales. It has been the slowest month for me since I began this journey in 2014. The last time I checked this month, I believe I had three sales. I have new projects on the horizon and a handful of loyal clients and customers who make up for the slow times that I may find myself in at any given moment. I do not regret being away in any way at all. I will never be sorry for doing what I feel is best for me. For too long, I have been selfless with my time, energy, and work load. This trip has taught me how to become a better version for myself and to those around me. The few friends I do have, they never ask more from me than I ask from myself. To have friends like that is worth more than the amount of money it takes to survive on this speck of dirt and rock. If I did not have them, I would not be able to be who I am today. It is okay to ask for help. To take time for yourself. To be selfish with any and every aspect of your life. No one will ever know what it takes and what it has taken for us to become who we are today. For us to be where we are today. I do not wake up expecting sympathy for my life and the past I have never looked back on since being this version of myself. Decency is a lost art in this time and place. Compassion is a forgotten skill several of us have not used since we were children. Since we saw the world as innocent as it saw us. I hope for better days all around. I hope mercy is something we can give to one another and not have to fucking cry out for it to some face(s) in the clouds or in our imagination. I will find my way. You will find yours. And I hope we all meet somewhere in the middle with how we feel about everything trying to destroy us. May love every know name and face. May grace know your limits. May empathy seek you out daily to embrace and comfort you. There is no easy way or right way to find your way through this life. I had been traveling basically the entire month of October. It is amazing how quickly it all rushes by you when you are where you feel you need to be. The airports, train stations, bus rides, and even renting a car in Milan, they have all taught me more than anyone and even more than my past years of road tripping to Utah and Arizona. Patience and resilience are real things. They are needed from the time you wake up, to the time you go to bed. I have never felt more free than walking through the streets of the small towns we found while over there. I remember walking through Time Square as an eighteen year old. Taking several trains all over the boroughs, and finding myself in my own world in each store I went into. Once you are able to find your center in this life, nothing or no one will ever be able to take it you from you. But it remains our job to make sure we locate it wherever we find ourselves. I hope this book helps you find yours. -MSTH